D0944953

THE PRUNING
WORD: *the parables of Flannery O'Connor*

THE PRUNING
WORD: *the parables of*
Flannery O'Connor

john r. may

UNIVERSITY
OF NOTRE DAME PRESS
NOTRE DAME & LONDON

Library of Congress Cataloging in Publication Data

May, John R
   The pruning word.

   Bibliography: p.
   1. O'Connor, Flannery—Criticism and interpretation.
I. Title.
PS3565.C57Z78   813'.5'4   75-19878
ISBN 0-268-01518-X

For Janet

χάρις, ἔλεος, εἰρήνη

In truth, in very truth I tell you,
  a time is coming,
indeed it is already here,
  when the dead shall hear the voice of the Son of God,
  and all who hear shall come to life.

John 5:25

Now, you have already been pruned by my words.

John 15:3 (J. B. Phillips trans.)

And for all this, nature is never spent;
  There lives the dearest freshness deep down things;
And though the last lights off the black West went
  Oh, morning, at the brown brink eastward, springs—
Because the Holy Ghost over the bent
  World broods with warm breast and with ah! bright wings.

Gerard Manley Hopkins, "God's Grandeur"

Contents

Acknowledgments

MY RESEARCH WAS SUPPORTED IN PART BY THE ACADEMIC Grant Fund of Loyola University of New Orleans.

I am deeply indebted to Robert Fitzgerald for allowing quotations from previously unpublished material found only in the Flannery O'Connor Collection; to Gerald Becham, Curator of the Collection, and Charles E. Beard, both of the Ina Dillard Russell Library, Georgia College, Milledgeville, for aiding my work there; to Kay Troendle and Mrs. Mildred Becnel for typing the manuscript at successive stages; and to my students in Religious Studies courses and seminars at Loyola University from 1971 to 1974 for the challenge of their enduring interest in O'Connor's fiction.

Special thanks are due to the editors of *Canadian Journal of Theology* (now *Studies in Religion/Sciences Religieuses*), *Southern Humanities Review, The Flannery O'Connor Bulletin,* and *Renascence* for permission to reuse material that appeared in their journals in quite different form: "Language-Event as Promise: Reflections on Theology and Literature," *Canadian Journal of Theology* 16: 3 & 4 (1970), 129–39; "The Pruning Word: Flannery O'Connor's Judgment of Intellectuals," *Southern Humanities Review* 4 (Fall 1970), 325–38; "Flannery O'Connor and the New Hermeneutic," *The Flannery O'Connor Bulletin* 2 (1973), 29–42; "Flannery O'Connor: Critical Consensus and the 'Objective' Interpretation," *Renascence* 27 (Summer 1975), 179–92.

Finally, I must acknowledge an inestimable debt of gratitude to Ann Rice for her editorial assistance in preparing yet another manuscript for publication.

Introduction

FLANNERY O'CONNOR WAS HARDLY A REVOLUTIONARY.
In her theory at least, if not her practice, she was reac-
tionary; yet, paradoxically, her sense of tradition in both
literature and religion has caused a revolution of sorts in
the American literary world. Although she may eventually
be judged a minor writer if undue emphasis is placed on
the size of her literary bequest, there are aspects of her
legacy that are unquestionably major. With considerable
art and no less determination, she confronted an increas-
ingly secular audience with religious, even specifically
Christian, concerns. "She is so recently dead," Robert
Drake observed, "one can't relegate the religion in her
stories to the safe distance of a Dante or Milton."[1] And,
one might add, so thoroughly American—and Southern—
that the cultural distance of a Mauriac or Greene will not
suffice either. The very fact that some two hundred essays
and at least ten books have appeared to date—a critical
reaction that is quantitatively staggering in relation to her
small body of works—may in itself suggest that we have
been dealing more with a crisis in literary criticism than
simply with the phenomenon of an exciting mid-twentieth-
century Southern writer.

We are faced with the acknowledged fact of her art,
inextricably—though uncomfortably, for many—bound to
her religious vision. The perplexing question her fiction has
raised challenges literary theorists as well as those committed to the practice of criticism. Perhaps it would be
more precise to say that, in forcing contemporary criticism
to witness a seemingly anachronistic wedding of art and
belief, she has asked whether the theoretically separable

can be separated in practice as well. What happens to our interpretations of her fiction if we decide in theory that we can accept her art and reject her religious belief? Can we avoid all reference to belief in our critical analyses of her stories, as some have tried, and still claim fidelity to the text? Is fictional language ever merely literary? Do we not strip O'Connor's art of its distinctive meaning if we fail to comprehend its grasp of mystery?[2]

Buried within some of the most perceptive and engaging studies of O'Connor's work are dangerous critical presuppositions that are ultimately the enemies of understanding. Critics and readers alike are forced to search for and admit these hidden assumptions (often as doctrinaire in their own way as O'Connor's vision seems to a secular world) in others' interpretations as well as in their own. Reading the O'Connor criticism one grows suspicious, not just of the evaluative judgments of others, but even of their analyses of a text. In addition to the aesthetic problem posed by the currently disturbing religious vision that O'Connor dramatizes, she has without a doubt raised the practical question of the very validity of our interpretations of fiction.

The expectation of achieving complete objectivity in the interpretation of literature as well as in our human understanding of reality is little more than a fantasy, and we are indebted to existential phenomenology for making this painfully clear to us. The supposed objectivity of the old creedal orthodoxy is as foreign to the 1970s as are the ages and men that produced it, however much O'Connor's theory sought to preserve this objectivity. Yet total subjectivity, the characteristic tendency of this age, is equally untenable as an alternative. In our common intellectual pursuits, we live in tension between the desire for objectivity and our innate tendency to subjectivism.

The quest for community of understanding involves more than a search for shared subjective understanding with others. The critical process itself would seem to imply a conviction that our analyses of a work, however tentative and temporary, do actually have something to do with the work itself, even if we are continually forced to the humble admission that the formulations of our interpretations are historically conditioned because they are wedded to language.

Between the objectivity of discernible form and the subjectivity of unique experience there is the "objectivity" of consensus. In the continuing debate over the question of validity in interpretation, far too little attention, it seems to me, is given to the existence of the community of scholarship. E.D. Hirsch's seminal study of interpretation speaks of consensus as the goal of valid interpretation. In the Preface to *Validity in Interpretation*, Hirsch expresses the hope "that the principles set forth in this book will help other interpreters gain confidence that consensus can be reached by mastering the relevant evidence—whether or not all of it is laid out in print."[3] Rather than consensus as the goal of a process which validates meaning through the discovery and verification of a "willed type" *in* the work, as Hirsch proposes, consensus is, I suggest, the result of a dialogue among scholars. The community that achieves the consensus is initially, at least, a community of shared interest, of intellectual honesty, of open dialogue. The consensus that emerges from their dialogue rests necessarily in a generally shared understanding of the work.

Such scholarly dialogue has been going on for centuries; one of the most obvious cases of progress toward consensus, and thus "objectivity," is in the area of biblical exegesis. The vast body of exegetical literature that has appeared, notably in the last century, represents as satisfactory an example of the process of consensus in interpretation as one can find within the limits of sacred or profane literature. What seems most admirable is that within the last few decades the quest for the "objective" interpretation has often, even in the most controversial texts of the Bible, overcome the biases of denominational belief.

The truly creative task of the critic of fiction is to
discover the aesthetic insight that orders the concrete
details of a work. He will thus be more inclined to demonstrate the overall design that harmonizes levels of meaning
in a story than to pick at bits and pieces like some
mechanical giant primed for destruction. Too much criticism, especially today when journals provide space in
abundance, is devoted to the work of evaluation. And
when evaluation is forthcoming too soon, as it does regrettably often, it is an indication perhaps that the critic has
confused his role with the reviewer's. I do not by any
means intend to disparage the evaluative function of the
critic, but only to insist that the work of thorough interpretation *must* precede it. The appraisal of a writer, especially where norms for judgment are extrinsic to literature,
may well be considered the critic's *prophetic* function by
comparison with the more creative work of integral interpretation. My concern here, however, once we have drawn
this obvious distinction between analysis and evaluation, is
exclusively with that analytical dialogue that leads to
"objectivity" in interpretation.

The "objective" interpretation that we seek, though
grounded in the work, is discovered within the order of
knowledge shared about the text. Although I realize that
my language is perilously close to the insinuation of an
order of existence, I do not appeal to the kind of
"intersubjective mode" that Wellek and Warren use to
explain the existence of the work of art itself.[4] I have
something far less metaphysical in mind. "Objective"
interpretation is actually *in* the body of analytical criticism, the collection of close readings that develops around
a particular writer and his work. While it is not spelled out
in so many words, it is there nevertheless in the critical
essays that continue to push back the horizon of obscurity
surrounding the meaning of a text.

An emerging consensus in interpretation can be readily
discerned, it seems to me, in the body of analytical essays
that is rapidly developing in response to Flannery O'Con-

nor's fiction. The three phases implicit in the critical dialogue are the following: the initial interpretation of the works, the evaluation of the criticism in relation to the works, and finally the so-called "reevaluation" of the works themselves. These are obviously not in reality distinct moments; they overlap in such a way that the second and third phases often begin, or at least appear to, before the work of initial interpretation has been completed. They are distinguishable, therefore, only through a process of abstraction based upon the achievement of certain levels of understanding.

The first phase is the most diffuse because of the variety of reactions a writer can prompt—and O'Connor obviously has more than proved the rule. What is commonly received as interpretation of a text may include anything from the essential reading of the text to casual labeling of literary types and groundless evaluations. Critics often seem amazingly innocent of theory. It is never more apparent than in their lack of awareness of how their presuppositions (psychological, social, philosophical, and theological) invariably shape, and even distort, their readings of a work. In an exceptionally revealing study, Allen D. Lackey classifies the critical response to Flannery O'Connor's fiction, and in describing what he considers to be the aim of the "objective critic," he enunciates a goal that lies close to the heart of my thesis. "The task of the objective critic," Lackey writes, "is to identify clearly his criteria for judgment without resorting to the subterfuge of presenting his own philosophy (or opposition to Miss O'Connor's theology) under the guise of objective literary criticism. The critic must have the integrity to acknowledge that his is at least partly subjective, not necessarily an objective reaction to the fiction being discussed. Only when such integrity is achieved can the output of any literary critic be considered a valuable addition to the literature of the field."[5] Although I wholeheartedly endorse the identification of criteria, I contend that the kind of integrity Lackey urges is achieved only through scholarly dialogue. Quite simply, critics need other critics to call them back to the evidence of the text—the challenge of the second stage.

Because of the hidden variety of critical assumptions, the first phase of the process toward consensus is the most subjective. Martha Stephens's *The Question of Flannery O'Connor*, though lately published (1973), clearly falls within this phase. The "question" of the title is actually the perennial "problem" of appreciation blocked by disbelief. For Stephens "A Good Man Is Hard to Find" is the representative instance in O'Connor of the discord between comedy and seriousness. Whereas Dorothy Walters in *Flannery O'Connor* (also 1973) allows the two to meld into the genre of tragicomedy, Stephens places a "tonal barrier" between them inasmuch as she contends that O'Connor's "unreasonable doctrine about human life" finds its dramatic expression in this otherwise humorous story's abruptly serious conclusion.[6] That Stephens's basic critical norm is philosophical rather than aesthetic becomes even more evident in her treatment of the novels. What she does, in effect, is use the rather nebulous literary category of "tone" to cloak the umbrage she takes at O'Connor's "stubborn refusal to see any good, any beauty or dignity or meaning, in ordinary human life."[7]

Insofar as one can speak of the completion of a phase, the first is not finished until each of the author's works has received the close reading that its uniqueness deserves. Although the interpretation of O'Connor's works is well into the second phase, the first is far from complete. Despite the volume of criticism, nearly half of her stories have not, in my estimation, received the close textual analysis they deserve.[8]

The second phase evaluates the criticism in relation to the works and seeks the aesthetic principle that harmonizes all the works; in it scholars are in dialogue with their peers over the body of interpretation that constitutes the first phase. Most often some of the best "close readings" of the text appear as reaction to earlier critical misinterpretation or to the omission of significant evidence. In this

way obscurities in textual interpretation are gradually
diminished and facile readings are rejected in favor of that
genuine ambiguity which is the touchstone of greatness.
Where the aesthetic cohesion of a whole body of fiction is
being considered, the dialogue of the second phase argues
for the uniqueness of the individual work against the
uncomfortable application of some generic type. Dialogue
exposes the presuppositions of critics and argues toward an
integral interpretation of the work as a unique blend of
part and whole. The literary consensus that most closely
parallels the growth of biblical exegesis results from the
gradual accumulation of convincing evidence related to a
theme.

The emerging consensus of the second phase may begin,
however, with only the negative assurance of what a text
does not mean, through the isolation and rejection of
tenuous opinions; yet affirmations frequently result from
negations. Although many of O'Connor's stories deal on
the literal level with the conflict between races and classes,
Miles Orvell in *Invisible Parade* expresses a clear consensus
of critical opinion when he writes, "She is dealing less with
the particulars of racial or social tensions than with the
universal occurrence of self-deception."[9] And the critics
now generally agree that O'Connor's work belongs not to
the school of Southern Gothic, but in the category of the
grotesque, and that her use of the grotesque is certainly
not gratuitous. No simple proportion between physical
deformity and spiritual grotesquerie can be found in
O'Connor's writing. In fact, the consensus that the two
stand in almost inverse proportion is most simply stated by
Robert Drake: "The real grotesques are the self-justified;
the apparent grotesques may be blessed."[10] Although
there are still explicitly contradictory opinions about
O'Connor's sense of history, a careful reading of the critics
indicates a certain agreement in their comments. Orvell,
linking O'Connor with the Southern tradition, insists that
"hers is not truly 'a historical fiction,'" whereas both
Drake and Kathleen Feeley, limiting their references to "A

Late Encounter with the Enemy," correctly imply that the basis of her healthy respect for history is theological rather than regional.[11]

Consensus also results from the synthesis of opposites as well as from the negation of an extreme. Preston M. Browning, Jr., in his *Flannery O'Connor*, offers a solution to the problem that has plagued O'Connor's critics ever since John Hawkes accused her of dabbling in the demonic for the sake of satire. Browning shows convincingly how the coincidence of opposites, the holy and the demonic, gives her work its peculiar power.[12] Furthermore, consensus through synthesis has demonstrated the balance in her fiction between faith and reason, matter and spirit. In retrospect, Stanley Edgar Hyman's judgment of O'Connor as "the most radical Christian dualist since Dostoevski" drew more attention than it deserved. "There are two of everything in her work," he writes, "one Christ's and one anti-Christ's."[13] Without specifically joining battle with Hyman, Carter Martin in *The True Country* provided an adequate early refutation of this unacceptable "dualistic" explanation in his demonstration of O'Connor's "sacramental view ... of reality" through which grace *and* matter are irrevocably joined; recently, though from a slightly different perspective, Browning has gently but unequivocally laid the charge to final rest.[14]

Works in concert, moreover, often complement one another like chamber musicians. Leon Driskell's and Joan T. Brittain's *The Eternal Crossroads*, proposing the arch as the structural frame of her fiction, represents an opposite swing of the pendulum from David Eggenschwiler's *The Christian Humanism of Flannery O'Connor*, which deals with the intellectual setting of the religious, psychological, and social dimensions of her works.[15] Forming a smooth transition between these poles are the combined religious and literary perspectives of Martin, Muller, Feeley, Orvell, and Walters.

A survey of the criticism of the stories in O'Connor's collections reveals that the endings of at least six stories (three in each collection) are still a source of substantial disagreement. There is considerable confusion, for example, about the nature of Thomas's judgment in "The Comforts of Home" as well as Mrs. May's in "Greenleaf." And no one, to my knowledge, has satisfactorily analyzed Sheppard's reaction to Norton's suicide in "The Lame Shall Enter First." Because of O'Connor's preoccupation with conversion, the strongest temptation, even among the most judicious critics, is to project actual conversion beyond the available evidence.[16]

In the final analysis when the problem of the religious dimension of O'Connor's fictional world is faced honestly, solutions still range from uneasy acceptance of the literary implications of her belief (Orvell) to rejection of her art where belief is too pronounced (Stephens). Where principles of aesthetic harmony are sought, there is the persistent temptation to accommodate a text at the expense of its uniqueness (Muller, Driskell and Brittain, Walters). A hermeneutic principle is of course no better than its recognized limits. Three of the book-length critics have avoided the unifying view and concerned themselves simply with the treatment of particular themes (Feeley, Eggenschwiler) or of themes and techniques (Martin). No one of them has attempted a close reading of all the short stories, and only three treat even the collected stories in any consistent detail (Feeley, Driskell and Brittain, Walters).

The phenomenon of the critical "reevaluation"—the third phase of the dialogue toward "objectivity"—requires close scrutiny in the light of these observations regarding consensus. From a publisher's point of view, and indeed a critic's, a sure way of selling one's product is to discover or offer the so-called new reading. I refer in theory to the "new" reading of a text that the established critical purists writing reviews for the prestigious journals always seem to be looking for and only rarely finding. *Any* acceptance of previous scholarship in a critical work often enough provokes an automatic *déjà vu* response. The very fact that they balk at not finding anything new is itself a kind of negative proof of the growth of consensus in interpretation.

Of all the critical books that have appeared to date, Josephine Hendin's *The World of Flannery O'Connor* alone would seem at first to fall within the category of the critical "reevaluation." Initially it is most engaging because of its starkly divergent perspective. Hendin even appears to be building on to the existing body of critical understanding when she asserts that "O'Connor told more than religious tales."[17] Yet the serious reviews of Hendin's work have rejected altogether—and rightly so—its psychological assumptions and reductionist conclusions. Even a critic like Stephens with her own severe reservations about O'Connor's view of man is outspoken against Hendin's reading of the works. "[Her] portrayal of O'Connor as a woman whose violent but deeply suppressed rejection of the role she was expected to play in southern society accounts for the belligerence—and what Hendin sees as the 'nihilism'—of her fiction is sometimes interesting," Stephens writes, "but one must reject altogether this critic's view of O'Connor's thought and hence her reading of the O'Connor works themselves."[18] One ought, it seems, to be as initially skeptical of the exclusive preoccupation with art as expression of psychic need as one is of art as expression of belief. For it is one thing to exclude the religious experience from consideration, as Hendin does, and another to advance a psychological interpretation that is diametrically opposed to the burden of critical conclusions to date. The principal reason, finally, for judging Hendin's analysis of O'Connor incompatible with the developing consensus is ultimately the only justifiable literary norm available to the critic; namely, the violence that her perspective does to the text.

Aside from "new" readings that are simply bad readings, putative "new" readings often result from the resolution of critical problems caused normally by the opaqueness of the literary text. Readings of this sort, rather than altering

the validity of previous scholarship, deepen our understanding of the work within the same language tradition
and thus deserve consideration in phase two of the
dialogical process. But where a reading is genuinely
new—and thus a critical "reevaluation" of this third
phase—how can we account for its newness? Authentic
reevaluations invariably result from the emergence of a
new language tradition.[19] The resultant reading represents
the encounter of a new philosophical tradition with the
author's work.

A plurality of contemporary language traditions has
assessed O'Connor's works from the beginning. Thus, with
little more than a decade elapsing since her death, we are
obviously too close to the completion of her work for the
possibility of reevaluation to arise. Examples of this third
phase though are not wanting in recent literary history.
The revival of interest in the Creole writer Kate Chopin is
undoubtedly best explained as a genuine reevaluation. The
Victorian world view of the earliest critics limited their
reading of *The Awakening* to a quest for sexual independence. The existentialist tradition provides a vision that
broadens the meaning of the novel to a parable about
man's frustrated search for freedom, without eliminating
the value of the more superficial sexual interpretation of
the work.[20] Whether or not Kate Chopin meant to say this
is at best irrelevant to the critical process. The language
itself bears the burden of expanded meaning. A genuine
new reading, therefore, must by definition *deepen* understanding rather than destroy the existing consensus. The
"reevaluation" of the third phase is actually a misnomer
for the "reinterpretation" of a writer's works.

"Objectivity" in interpretation, as the phases of critical
reaction to Flannery O'Connor illustrate, lies in the
direction of consensus within the community of literary
critics. The dialogue in question has at its best constantly
called critics back to the concrete details of her stories. A
survey of O'Connor's critics shows clearly that the two
principal sources of continuing debate lie in the tension

between art and belief and in the attempt at harmonizing the whole and its parts. Since critical consensus seeks finally not only to unify the whole with its parts but also to explore the limits of meaning in an author, the last word in the dialogue over O'Connor's achievement has obviously not been spoken.

Prior to proposing a resolution to these enduring tensions, I have first sought to locate assurance concerning the correct reading of her stories within the broader context of the process of consensus that literary criticism seems normally to follow. A selected bibliography of textual analyses from the journals is offered here not only as demonstration of the effect of scholarly dialogue but also to assist students of O'Connor in the already difficult task of controlling the secondary sources concerned simply with interpretation.

The aesthetic principle that orchestrates the whole of O'Connor's fiction while allowing the individual works to appear in their maximum uniqueness is to be found, I propose, in the New Hermeneutic's understanding of "word" as interpreter of human existence (chapter 1). Whereas O'Connor's own literary theory is principally concerned with the relationship between the work of art and external reality (which, for her, is ultimately "mystery"), her fiction achieves its distinctive dramatic impact through the power of language to interpret its listener rather than through its need to be interpreted by him. The word of revelation spoken or the gesture of judgment seen constitutes the dramatic core of O'Connor's narratives and articulates their meaning for the reader.

The word-orientation of O'Connor's fiction, moreover, is basically scriptural in inspiration and parabolic in effect. The specific New Testament literary form that her art imitates is the parable, where religious meaning is structured in terms of human conflict symbolizing man's relationship with God. For what the parables of Jesus reveal to the listener is that life is gained or lost in the midst of everyday existence. Thus, the problem of art and belief in O'Connor is resolved, at least on the level of interpretation, when the reader-critic realizes that the often harsh, specifically Christian theology of O'Connor's fiction constitutes its countryside (the literal level) whereas its true country (the level of meaning) employs the hermeneutic word of radical human respect for mystery. The reader has no choice but to hear the universal language of *homo religiosus* spoken by her contemporary parables, and no valid interpretation of them can avoid at least the literary analogues of their basic religious language—poverty, possibility, and judgment.

Moreover, as a structural aesthetic principle that varies from narrative to narrative, the interpreting word permits each short story and novel to mediate its own specific insight into the mystery of existence (chapters 2–4) and thus preserves perfectly the uniqueness of the individual text. If in the final analysis the overall configuration of meaning that the parables produce suggests rather than states a religious view that is Christian, each story is no more integrally Christian in meaning than the parables of Jesus taken singly. The prophetic voice that O'Connor dares to imitate—with acknowledged success—speaks with eschatological urgency, yet with simplicity, of the poverty of man. Audacious enough to judge the modern world with her own "pruning word," she reluctantly but realistically accepted the probability that her work—like the parables of Jesus—would be rejected. The reader should, however, understand precisely what he is rejecting—not orthodox Christian theology in its fullness but a single-minded revelation of human limitation and possibility in the face of mystery.

The quotations from O'Connor's fiction, made without distracting page references, are from the original editions of the novels (*Wise Blood*, New York: Harcourt, Brace and Co., 1952; *The Violent Bear It Away*, New York: Farrar, Straus and Cudahy, 1960) and *The Complete Stories* (New York: Farrar, Straus and Giroux, 1971).

1: The New Hermeneutic and the Parables of Jesus

BEHIND THE CONTEMPORARY CRITIC'S STRUGGLE WITH the unavoidable evidence of faith in Flannery O'Connor's fiction lies the theoretical problem of the relationship between art and belief, and for more than two decades now scholars—stimulated by the New Critical concern for form over content in literature—have sought new ways to resolve that tension in a pluralistic world.[1] The most interesting developments in the search for a common ground between literature and religion have undoubtedly been in the area of philosophy of language, since language is obviously common to both. Specifically, it is the interpretive function of language, as understood in the New Hermeneutic, that provides not only an acceptable theoretical explanation of faith's relationship to art, but also a suitable heuristic principle for the analysis of O'Connor's fiction.

For proponents of the New Hermeneutic, such as Gerhard Ebeling and Ernst Fuchs, reality is present to us in language; the world in which we live is largely inherited through the language tradition that is passed on to us. (Language includes all that Martin Heidegger calls "primordial discourse"—word, gesture, deed, and even silence.) Because the world embraces self, the understanding of world which we inherit includes self-understanding. This self-understanding, transmitted by language, is constantly thrown into question by our own fresh experience of

1

reality. New experience may or may not involve a shift in
self-understanding; when it does, there arises a major crisis
of language, because the new self-understanding constitutes a break with the inherited common understanding
that was the basis of dialogue. Ebeling writes: "The fact of
reality's confronting me and the manner in which it does
so are conditioned by the language spoken to me. And
again, the understanding of language spoken to me, together with my own ways of using language, are conditioned
by the way in which reality confronts me and the manner
in which I let myself be confronted by it."[2]

The agony caused by a breakdown of common understanding will be painfully obvious to anyone who is
familiar with the current theological crisis within the
Roman Catholic Church. The language tradition which had
survived since the Council of Trent and through which the
reality of the sacramental life of the Church was transmitted to the young until Vatican Council II was one that
presented the sacraments as physical causes of grace and
men as primarily passive recipients of that grace. A fresh
confrontation of the personal dimension of worship has
produced a language of encounter, which has resulted in a
radically new understanding of the sacraments and man's
active, personal participation in ritual.[3] Thus a dialogical
rift of major proportions has ensued; the old language no
longer speaks reality to the young. We can readily see,
therefore, how we fall prey to a language tradition unless
we investigate the history of that tradition or dispose
ourselves to reality in a new way; both investigation and
disposition have played an important part in the development of this new tradition in sacramental theology.

Where there is shared common understanding, we
experience language as event—the power of speech to
create unity. For through language we expose our mental
images to agreement or contradiction by others. Language-
event can consist either in the imparting of information or
in sharing. When information is imparted, man experiences
a thing and he is cast in the role of observer. When there is

sharing, man experiences a personal benefit: something happens to him because he has shared an encounter. Only in this latter sense of sharing can language-event truly be considered communication. "Word is therefore rightly understood," says Ebeling, "when it is viewed as an event which—like love—involves at least two. The basic structure of word is therefore not statement—that is an abstract variety of the word-event—but apprisal, certainly not in the colorless sense of information, but in the pregnant sense of participation and communication."[4]

In the strict signification of the Hebrew *dabar* (word), language is also "happening word." It is not enough, Ebeling insists, "to inquire into [language's] intrinsic meaning, but that must be joined up with the question of its future, of what it effects."[5] Language as event, therefore, is both meaning and power—meaning because it implies a shared understanding, and power because it effects a response from man, it sets him in motion, it discloses a future. Man exists "linguistically" between call and response. The word is spoken to him; it not only urges a response, it actually gives the power to respond. And the word that is spoken is, according to Ernst Fuchs, an announcement of time, of "what it is time for."[6]

Thus, language is also promise. It is most surely promise when it announces what has not yet come to be in such a way that future possibility is present to us as a hope that can be realized. The speaker pledges and imparts himself to the other and opens a future to him by awakening a genuine hope within him.

For the believer, the Word of God is authentic language that both announces what it is time for and gives the power to respond. It is important to note here that God's Word announces time and power, not because it is God's, but precisely because it is word. The incontestable authenticity of that Word and the efficacy of its power, however, are dependent upon God's presence in the Word. It brings a new language tradition into existence out of which man can live. If language is gift that gives birth to

man's self-understanding, God's Word is gift that gives
birth to the self-understanding of faith.

The traditional approach to God's Word has been that,
owing to its opaqueness, it requires interpretation—based
originally no doubt on the assumption that verbal statements pose the problem of understanding. Ebeling insists—
and this is the fundamental divergence of the New
Hermeneutic—that the assumption concerning the need for
interpreting God's Word was a fundamental misunder-
standing of the nature of language:

> The primary phenomenon in the realm of understanding
> is not understanding *of* language but understanding
> *through* language. The word is not really the
> object of understanding, and thus the thing that
> poses the problem of understanding, the solution
> of which requires exposition and therefore also her-
> meneutics as the theory of understanding. Rather,
> the word is what opens up and mediates understanding
> i.e., brings something to understanding. *The word itself
> has a hermeneutic function.* If the word-event takes
> place normally, i.e., according to its appointed purpose,
> then there is no need of any aid to understanding, but it
> is itself an aid to understanding.[7]

Interpretation is required, therefore, *only* where
language-event is impeded for some reason or other. The
function of hermeneutics is to make room for the word's
own hermeneutic function; it serves the word's intelligi-
bility. The text wants to speak to man because it is
language. This is its proper vocation. And if, in the final
analysis, man is to be interpreted by the text—the
possibilities of his situation to be illumined by it—it is the
task of the interpreter to place the text where it speaks to
man. Its proper place is where it becomes language-event
for him, where understanding is shared and unity effected.
Thus the interpreter's role is clearly ancillary to the text,
for the language of the text has priority over the thought
of the interpreter.

Now, one may readily grant the need for interpreting God's Word in order for it to become event for us (because of the philological and historical problems that obviously impede its own hermeneutical function), yet question the necessity of interpretation where the human language of literature is concerned. Those who write principally in a subjectivist phenomenological vein, emphasizing the *experience* of literature, often seem to deprecate the process of interpretation. Moreover, the language of literature is, in a very special sense, authentic language—"the voice of being naming itself through the mouth of the poet."[8] In fact, as Robert Funk explains Heidegger, "the primordial function of language is understood best by the true poets. . . . The poet names being and so brings it to stand. Being calls to man, and in responding he, in turn, calls being out of chaos, so to speak, by giving it a place to dwell in language."[9] The language of literature, described by Victor Shklovsky and Boris Eichenbaum in terms of "defamiliarization" and "roughened form," is a means, Eichenbaum says, "of destroying the automatism of perception."[10] Yet, the same grammatical and historical problems obviously arise with literature as well as with God's word. Moreover, aesthetic language is by nature so complex and controlled that the inexperienced reader misses the nuances, if not the basic sense, of literature without the help of a skillful exposure of its constitutive elements. "Roughened form" actually implies distance from the uninitiated. In "Writing Short Stories," Flannery O'Connor hinted at the necessity of interpretation while describing its ancillary function: "The meaning of fiction is not abstract meaning but experienced meaning, and the purpose of making statements about the meaning of a story is only to help you to experience that meaning more fully."[11]

Contemporary language theory, as we have seen, is principally concerned with the effect of language upon its audience: what language communicates when it is event for the listener or reader. Traditionally, though, there have been three elements in the hermeneutical process—reality, the work, and the audience. The first moment of the

sequence of interpretation raises the question of the
relationship between the language of the work of art and
external reality; the second moment, as we have seen in
detail, poses the problematic of understanding or communication, how language affects its audience or is
affected by it. In her essays in literary theory, Flannery
O'Connor places the emphasis in the hermeneutical process
on its first moment, the relationship between the language
of the work and reality.

Although she undoubtedly appreciates the creative role
of the writer, it is clear from her theory of literature that
whatever freedom she grants the writer in selecting and
shaping his material is firmly limited by the demands of a
strict theological realism. In "The Church and the Fiction
Writer," she speaks about the "what-is" that is the
concrete material of the writer: "The writer learns,
perhaps more quickly than the reader, to be humble in the
face of what-is. What-is is all he has to do with; the
concrete is his medium; and he will realize eventually that
fiction can transcend its limitations only by staying within
them" (*Mystery and Manners*, p. 146). Again in her talk
entitled "Writing Short Stories," she addresses herself
more specifically to the way the writer works with reality:
"The first and most obvious characteristic of fiction is that
it deals with reality through what can be seen, heard,
smelt, tasted, and touched" (p. 91). Yet, because appearance is obviously not the same as reality, she concedes that
"we must give the artist the liberty to make certain
rearrangements of nature if these will lead to greater
depths of vision" (p. 98). Her theological realism is never
more apparent than in this discussion of the writer's
freedom to shape reality to his purposes, for she concludes
emphatically: "The artist himself always has to remember
that what he is rearranging *is* nature, and that he has to
know it and be able to describe it accurately in order to
have the authority to rearrange it at all" (p. 98).

The ultimate purpose of the artist's use of concrete
reality is, as she sees it, to transcend that reality through

vision. "The peculiar problem of the short-story writer," she asserts, "is how to make the action he describes reveal as much of the mystery of existence as possible. He has only a short space to do it in and he can't do it by statement. He has to do it by showing, not by saying, and by showing the concrete—so that his problem is really how to make the concrete work double time for him" (p. 98). For O'Connor, the mystery of existence discloses a transcendent world that is every bit as real as the visible world. "The realism of each novelist," she says, "will depend on his view of the ultimate reaches of reality. . . . What he sees on the surface will be of interest to him only as he can go through it into an experience of mystery itself" (pp. 40—41). Relating the problems of grotesque fiction to her understanding of the reality of mystery, she remarks: "[The writer] is looking for one image that will connect or combine two points; one is a point in the concrete, and the other is a point not visible to the naked eye, but believed in by him firmly, just as real to him, really, as the one that everybody sees" (p. 42). This theological realism stems, of course, from an orthodox Christian vision—Flannery O'Connor's acknowledged Roman Catholic faith.

The novelist as a "realist of distances," who has this capacity "of seeing near things with their extensions of meaning and thus of seeing far things close up" (p. 44), is basically prophetic. The concrete works "double time" for him because moral judgment is part of the very act of seeing. "The way of drama," she writes, "[is] that with one stroke the writer has both to mirror and judge" (p. 117). Elsewhere she states: "For the fiction writer, everything has its testing point in the eye, and the eye is an organ that eventually involves the whole personality, and as much of the world as can be got into it. It involves judgment. Judgment is something that begins in the act of vision, and when it does not, or when it becomes separated from vision, then a confusion exists in the mind which transfers itself to the story" (p. 91). "The writer's moral sense," she concludes, "coincides with his dramatic sense, and I see no way for it to do this unless his moral judgment is part of the very act of seeing" (p. 31). Belief in Christian dogma, moreover, is not only not a hindrance to the writer, it actually "frees the storyteller to observe . . . by guaranteeing his respect for mystery" (p. 31). Indeed, faith is the light itself by which the writer sees; it does not, however, dictate what he sees. "Your beliefs will be the light by which you see," she insists, "but they will not be what you see and they will not be a substitute for seeing" (p. 91).

The location of that "peculiar crossroads where time and place and eternity somehow meet" (p. 59) is the special problem of the fiction writer; it means intimate knowledge of a region, its people and their manners. "The country, with its body of manners, that he knows well enough to describe" (p. 28) is the writer's "countryside." For even though he is literally free to choose whatever he wants to write about, "he cannot choose what he is able to make live" (p. 27). A writer gets "the sense of manners . . . from the texture of experience that surrounds [him] " (p. 103). "Manners" becomes for O'Connor a simple synonym for the concrete material of dramatic action; in the hands of the fiction writer, manners are "those conventions which . . . reveal that central mystery [of our position on earth] " (p. 124). "Through the concrete particulars of a life that he can make believable," the fiction writer's country expands from the "countryside" that he knows to the "true country" that he believes in—"which the writer with Christian conviction will consider to be what is eternal and absolute" (p. 27).

It is within the context of her discussion of manners, of the writer's familiarity with his region, that O'Connor shifts to a consideration of the second moment of the hermeneutical process. The writer leaves his region, she says, "at great peril to that balance between principle and fact, between judgment and observation, which is so necessary to maintain if fiction is to be true." For, "unless the novelist has gone utterly out of his mind, his aim is still communication, and communication suggests talking inside a community" (pp. 53–54). She assumes, therefore, that the artist wishes to communicate. She does not, however, offer as detailed an explanation of the process of communication as she does of the relationship between the work and the reality it mirrors. In addition to her insistence that communication works best within the community of those who share the same manners, she speaks of the artist's communication of his prophetic vision as revelation to the reader, provided the latter sees the creative process as basically healthy. "Those who believe that art proceeds from a healthy, and not from a diseased, faculty of the mind," she writes, "will take what [the artist] shows them as a revelation, not of what we ought to be but of what we are at a given time and under given circumstances; that is, as a limited revelation but revelation nevertheless" (p. 34).

The revelation that O'Connor considers basic to the task of the fiction writer is undoubtedly that of radical poverty. "His concern with poverty," she observes, "is with a poverty fundamental to man. I believe that the basic experience of everyone is the experience of human limitation" (p. 131). Now if the writer's audience is attuned to his concerns, then the revelation is a matter of simple communication; but where the same vision is not shared, he must shock his audience with this revelation of limitation. The grotesque in Flannery O'Connor is thus a technique of communication. "The novelist with Christian concerns will find in modern life distortions which are repugnant to him," she insists, "and his problem will be to make these appear as distortions to an audience which is used to seeing them as natural; and he may well be forced to take ever more violent means to get his vision across to his hostile audience. . . . To the hard of hearing you shout, and for the almost-blind you draw large and startling figures" (pp. 33–34).

The threefold hermeneutical sequence implied in O'Connor's theory of fiction offers, then, these variations on the traditional elements: reality as manners *and* mystery (countryside *and* true country), the presentation of a dramatic reality as composite of vision and judgment, and finally meaning or communication as startling revelation. In her critical essays she clearly places the main emphasis on the first moment of the process, the relationship between the story and ultimate reality. It is evident and reasonable that her theological realism would dictate her concern with how and what the writer "sees"; she was after all called upon in her public appearances to reflect upon *her* experience as a creative writer. This preoccupation of her theory is confirmed of course by the title her editors, Sally and Robert Fitzgerald, aptly chose for the posthumous collection of essays—*Mystery and Manners.*

Such a theological realism, typical perhaps of traditional criticism is far from the nominalism of the New Critics and the New Hermeneuts. The New Hermeneutic insists that the primary function relative to God's Word is not interpreting It, but allowing It to interpret us, to illumine our existence. It seeks to avoid the subjectivism of historical criticism by placing the ultimate power to interpret in the word itself. As Gerhard Ebeling has expressed it, *"the text* [of Sacred Scripture] *by means of the sermon becomes a hermeneutic aid in the understanding of present experience.* Where that happens radically, there true word is uttered, and that in fact means God's Word."[12] The reason for the word's unintelligibility, as we have seen, is not the opaqueness of the text, but rather of our own situation. It is our own present condition then that must be illumined.

The New Critics, emphasizing the form of the work of art and the relationship of form to meaning, minimize or disregard altogether the work's relationship to reality. It is the pattern or structure of the work's "world," made up of plot, characters, setting, world view, and tone, that "we must scrutinize when we attempt to compare a novel with life or to judge, ethically or socially, a novelist's work."[13]

In answer to the question "What does the poem mean or say?," Eliseo Vivas writes:

> What it means is not a world it reflects, or imitates, or represents in illusion, in the sense of a world as envisaged by the mind prior to the poetic activity in the manner in which it is envisaged in poetry. What the poem says or means is the world it reveals or discloses *in* and *through* itself, a new world, whose features prior to the act of poetic revelation, were concealed from us. . . . What the poem says or means—or, in other words, the object of the poem—is, genetically speaking, the full-bodied, value-freighted, ordered, self-sufficient . world it presents to us for the first time.[14]

R.W.B. Lewis describes the new creation that the world of the work of art is in these terms: "They are 'transcendental world-views' created by the very play and pressure of the images invoked. They may contain occasionally the essences of some long-gone pieties; but their vitality is new, their foliation original."[15] The world of a literary work can be compared with the world that we know to determine whether it is true to reality *only* insofar as—and this is the attenuated realism of the New Critics—it conforms to the "form of human experience."[16] If it reflects the tensions and stresses, the possibilities and complexities of life as we experience it, then it can indeed be called *true*.

Yet, even though the emphasis in O'Connor's *theory* is world's apart from these recent literary and hermeneutical trends, her *fiction* tells a different story, so to speak. A close reading of the structural dynamism of her short stories and novels indicates that she had, if not wanted, the best of both worlds. For whereas traditional hermeneutic theory explains her understanding of the relationship between the work and reality, the New Hermeneutic is the key to understanding the religious dimension of the aesthetic function of her stories, the relationship between the work and meaning. And it is this realization, I believe, that opens up the possibility of a workable solution to the continuing critical debate over the tension between art and belief in O'Connor's works. The question of her world view, so well known from her lectures in theory and her defense of the Catholic writer, is significant only to the extent it reveals itself in the dramatic structure of the story. For word as understood in the New Hermeneutic is radically human—and therefore possibly religious rather than specifically Christian—inasmuch as it mediates all reality, even mystery, to the listener. As word the stories can illumine the reader's existence; that is the power of language itself. They at least challenge him to respond.

O'Connor's short story "Revelation" is prototypical of the hermeneutical function of language and of a literary text, and brief reference to it here will no doubt help to illustrate this new understanding of language and to set the stage for the following chapters. The protagonist, Mrs. Turpin, is a good woman whose one shortcoming apparently is that she has constructed an artificial hierarchy of social classes in which she can place anyone she meets. She pities white-trash and Negroes, who are obviously less well off than she is, because they cannot seem to make anything of themselves or do anything with what is given to them. The conflict in the story results from the confrontation of her condescending social philosophy with the revealing word of judgment spoken to her by Mary Grace, who calls her an "old wart hog" and tells her to go back to hell where she came from. Mary Grace, as her name itself suggests, announces the time of repentance. Ruby Turpin is thus suspended between word and response, between judgment and acceptance. The word of judgment interprets her because it clearly places her where she has placed white-trash and Negroes—last! Before she can accept the judgment leveled against her, she goes through the tortures of a self-righteous Job. But she does eventually respond; the word effects her acceptance of a new vision of reality and the ordering of classes. The authentic language of judgment is spoken to her, and it brings forth new life by announcing its possibility. Her encounter with Mary Grace is event and promise.

Although Mrs. Turpin tries initially to interpret the word, to remove its sting, she eventually allows it to interpret her, to shatter her illusions of superiority to "trashy" people—the folly of her social condescension based on material possessions. Flannery O'Connor has given brilliant contemporary expression to Jesus' teaching that the first shall be last and the last first. But we have until now discussed only the hermeneutical function of the word *within* the story. The story itself speaks this word of judgment to the reader. It interprets as well the folly of our own human tendency to determine—rather than discover—reality's order, to consider ourselves superior to others, to impose our ways on others. It forces us, through the shared experience of Mrs. Turpin's ordeal, to accept the fact that the word must interpret us, not we the word.

To specify precisely *how* O'Connor's stories work, in the light of the New Hermeneutic, we must appeal to the literary form of the Word in Scripture which most closely approximates, if not adequately corresponds to, the fictional form she uses. That scriptural form is of course the parable. Meaning in O'Connor's fiction like meaning in the parables of Jesus is accurately expressed only in terms of universal human experience. If their meaning is fundamentally religious, it is because they confront man with his radical poverty in the face of reality. They startle him with the suddenness of the sacred in the midst of the ordinary. "The parables' existential understanding," Dan Otto Via explains, "is that existence is gained or lost in the midst of ordinary life."[17]

The parables of Jesus are certainly not religious because they employ language that is specifically Christian. Aside from being the basest sort of anachronism, this would have defeated the purpose of Jesus' preaching, his audience would have lacked the capacity to comprehend or been offended beyond comprehension. A new language tradition comes into existence, not because a wholly new terminology is used, but through a new configuration of existing language that forces us to take a fresh look at our world because it makes reality live for us in a new way. Except for the parable of the Sower (Mark 4:3–8, 14–20; Matt. 13:3–8, 19–23; Luke 8:5–8, 11–15) which the synoptic evangelists explicitly interpret as an allegory of the relationship between God and man (and possibly also Luke's parable of the Pounds, 19:12–27), the parables of Jesus are not allegories but dramatic narratives involving conflicts between human beings that symbolize rather than describe man's relationship to ultimate reality. I am referring of course to what Via calls Jesus' parables in the narrow sense, rather than to either the similitude or the example story.[18] The example stories (e.g., the Good Samaritan, the Pharisee and the Publican) tell us exactly what we should do or avoid; the similitude (e.g., the Lost Coin, the Pearl Merchant) presents a familiar image, a typical, recurring scene from everyday life, and thus has its effect by appealing to what is universally acknowledged. For Via the parable in the narrow sense is "a freely invented story told with a series of verbs in the past tense" (e.g., the Prodigal Son, the Talents, the Unjust Steward).[19] It is not concerned with the typical, but with "making the particular credible and probable."[20] In the parable strictly conceived, therefore, as in fiction, "we have a story which is analogous to, which points to but is not identical with, a situation or world of thought outside of the story."[21]

The parable achieves its effect aesthetically; that is, symbolically, figuratively, indirectly. The aesthetic nature of the parables is implied in the synoptic evangelists' recurring comment on the ambiguity with which they were received. The most extreme position is the suggestion in Mark 4:11–12 that Jesus taught in parables purposely to conceal the truth from those predestined to remain in their sins: "To you the secret of the kingdom of God has been given; but to those who are outside everything comes by way of parables, so that (as Scripture says) they may look and look, but see nothing; they may hear and hear, but understand nothing; otherwise they might turn to God and be forgiven."[22] A more benign interpretation of this passage, but still in accord with the symbolic mode that parables represent (and curiously apropos of O'Connor's sentiments about the "modern" reader), would be that the indirect appeal of the parables provides the hardened of heart with an excuse for not understanding. Moreover, since this text is joined to an explanation of the parable for "the Twelve and others," it is possibly a reflection of the theme of the Messianic secret in Mark, in which the parables become a device for concealing the teaching of the kingdom from the uninitiated until the time when the Son of Man is revealed to all. Aside from this one perplexing text in Mark, there is sufficient evidence elsewhere in the synoptic Gospels that Jesus intended the parables to be heard and understood, as in the varied repetition of the command "If you have ears to hear, then hear" (Mark 4:9, 30; 7:14; 12:9; Matt. 18:12; 21:28; Luke 6:47; 13:18). So if we take the parables as "freely invented stories" to be understood, we will conclude with Via that "the many elements of the parable *within* their pattern of connections as a *whole* do imply an understanding of existence which may be related in some way both to the world of ideas outside of the parable and to the historical situation in which it arose."[23]

Inasmuch as the parable in a narrow sense thrives on the drama of human encounter as a figurative expression of the drama between God and man, it uses ordinary human language, rather than specifically theological terms, to mediate the ultimate reaches of reality to man. Reflecting the historical situation of their author, the parables proclaim what it means to exist in a boundary situation, how the eschatological crisis occurs within the confines of everyday existence.[24] Although we do not know whether she realized the formal similarities between her fiction and the parables of Jesus, O'Connor used language to describe her art that coincides perfectly with this interpretation of the purpose of the parables. The eschatological crisis is

indeed, in O'Connor's words, that "mysterious passage
past [the dragon], or into his jaws, that stories of any
depth will always be concerned to tell."[25] The characteristic violence of her tales reflects "the extreme situation
that best reveals what we are essentially."[26]

"Revelation," like the best of O'Connor's fiction, is a
disquieting contemporary parable. Its parabolic meaning is
quite simply, as Robert Funk has demonstrated concerning
the parables of Jesus, that the Pharisee is the one who
insists that he is the interpreter of the word, whereas the
sinner allows himself to be interpreted by it. "Grace",
Funk writes, "always wounds from behind, at the point
where man thinks he is least vulnerable. Grace is harder
than man thinks: he moralizes judgment in order to take
the edge off it. Grace is more indulgent than man thinks:
but it is never indulgent at the point where he thinks it
ought to be indulgent."[27]

Even though it is evident that Flannery O'Connor read
widely in philosophy and theology, there is little indication that she was familiar with the New Hermeneutic as
such. Kathleen Feeley's *Flannery O'Connor: Voice of the
Peacock*, which explores the relationship between her
"eclectic" reading and the themes that emerge in her
fiction, provides a bibliography of the principal source
books from her library.[28] O'Connor marked and used (in
"Good Country People") Heidegger's *Existence and Being*;
it is however the so-called later Heidegger of *Being and
Time* who is relevant to the New Hermeneutic. The works
of Gerhard Ebeling and Ernst Fuchs are too recent, at least
in translation, to have been part of her reading. And Dan
Otto Via's *The Parables: Their Literary and Existential
Dimension* was published after her death.

But she was a devoted student of the Bible, and works
like Jean Levie's *The Bible, Word of God in Words of Men*
and Bruce Vawter's *The Conscience of Israel: Pre-exilic
Prophets and Prophecy*, both of which she read, marked
and reviewed for the Georgia Catholic newspaper, could
have helped focus her preoccupation with the power of

language that reading the Bible was already beginning to shape.[29] In its day Levie's work was a milestone in popular Catholic literature on the Bible. Assuming with the best exegetical tradition that "it is *through men* that God speaks to us,"[30] Levie introduces his reader to the process whereby one goes from the human word of Scripture to an understanding of the divine message. He provides a history of recent developments in archeology and biblical criticism as well as a lucid modern explanation of the doctrine of inspiration. Vawter's *The Conscience of Israel*, as its subtitle indicates, considers the nature and practice of prophecy in Israel before the Babylonian exile. The title captures perfectly Vawter's thesis that "the chief function of the prophet was to reveal the moral will of God to a disobedient people."[31] Far from confusing prophecy with prediction of future events (a popular fallacy), O'Connor understood that the prophet interprets events in the light of the covenant, announcing God's judgment of the people's sins and His call to fidelity. An action or gesture of the prophet, as Vawter explains, often accompanies or replaces his words (e.g., Jeremiah's yoke and Isaiah's nakedness), a mode of prophetic symbolism that O'Connor frequently employed. With reading such as this, it is no wonder that she links judgment with vision in her understanding of the prophetic role of the Catholic fiction writer.

Although questions of specific indebtedness are beyond my concern here, it is clear enough that the depth of O'Connor's faith and the biblical obsession of her region provided the general foundation for her preference for a fictional world graced with revealing language. What assurance though does awareness of the hermeneutic core of her parables offer the critic in view of the continuing debate over art and belief? The specifics of religious belief can threaten not only the equity of evaluation and the serenity of the aesthetic experience but also, as we noted, the validity of interpretation itself. The latter remains our principal concern here.[32]

The task that the interpreter faces is obviously not one
of enunciating the breadth of the detailed Christian
topography of her fictional countryside; least of all is it a
matter of using her known commitment to Catholicism or
her essays in literary theory, which are so clearly informed
by faith, as a heuristic device for reading the stories.
Actually, the interpreter lays aside the particulars of belief
in order to expose the structural dimensions of the work's
view of man. The crucial question related to the meaning
of O'Connor's fiction deals with the centrality of its
interpretive language. The parabolic form dictates the
religious limits of that language; the hermeneutic core of
her narratives guides the interpreter to their meaning and
specifies the awareness they call the reader to as word. The
meaning of the dramatic human conflict at the heart of her
parables must be expressed in the universal human
language of limitation, possibility and judgment, which
supersedes the confessional language of explicit Christianity, just as the true country ultimately replaces the
countryside and higher levels of meaning transcend the
literal. When O'Connor admits that one does not have to
be a Catholic to write a Catholic novel, she herself
abandons the explicitly theological terminology of "the
Fall, the Redemption, and the Judgment"[33] and appeals
to their human, existential analogues. The Catholic novel,
she says, "cannot see man as determined; it cannot see him
as totally depraved. It will see him as incomplete in
himself, as prone to evil, but as redeemable when his own
efforts are assisted by grace. And it will see this grace as
working through nature, but as entirely transcending it, so
that a door is always open to possibility and the
unexpected in the human soul."[34] This moment of grace
on the human level is characterized by the surprise of unexpected possibility, often the shock of violent judgment.

While Christian fundamentalism is the concrete dimension of O'Connor's countryside, openness to mystery in its
revelation of radical human poverty is the hermeneutic of
her true country. The primordial religious word of

revelation spoken to the protagonist interprets our existential situation. The reader, aided by the critic's preparatory analysis, needs only to submit himself to the power of parabolic language. The language of her parables instructs the reader to acknowledge that he is not the measure of all things. It cannot demand this assent; no language can. But inasmuch as the reader exists between call and response, O'Connor's fiction as word is challenging him to respect the radical mystery of existence; to rob her stories of this *meaning* is to destroy their parabolic art.

If the total configuration of her fictional world is more compatible with a Christian view of human existence than with any other particular vision of religious man—and it obviously is—the individual stories and novels, like the parables of Jesus taken singly, never mediate a total vision. Not even on the subjective level of aesthetic experience, therefore, where the non-analytic, direct response comes closest to exposing the reader to the integral emotional impact of the world of her works, can O'Connor's fiction demand assent to Christianity; in this instance too it is never more than—but always at least—word. Perhaps what critics and readers of differing persuasions fear, without necessarily knowing why, is the seductive power of word; but more often than not, if the reaction of Jesus' contemporaries to his parables is any omen, this authentic language alienates rather than seduces.

Concretely speaking, then, the task of the interpreter —which I insist must always be considered as ancillary to the hermeneutical function of the text itself—is to disclose, to the best of his ability, the word and/or gesture which constitute(s) the dramatic center of the literary work. While introducing a reading of "A Good Man Is Hard to Find" at Hollins College, Virginia (1963), O'Connor discussed the effectiveness of a story in terms that are directly related to the interpretive role of language. "I often ask myself," she said, "what makes a story work, and what makes it hold up as a story, and I have decided that it is probably some action, some gesture of a character that is unlike any other in the story, one which indicates where the real heart of the story lies. This would have to be an action or a gesture which was both totally right and totally unexpected; it would have to be one that was both in character and beyond character; it would have to suggest both the world and eternity."[35] Concerning the grandmother's climactic recognition of The Misfit, she insisted: "I think myself that if I took out this gesture and what she says with it, I would have no story. What was left would not be worth your attention."[36]

Despite the fact that it is obviously easier to locate the dramatic center of a short story in terms of word and gesture, it is my contention that language functions the same way in O'Connor's novels as well. The dramatic center of Flannery O'Connor's fiction is invariably the word of revelation spoken to the protagonist that either achieves conversion or announces simple condemnation. This word also invariably sheds light upon the meaning of the story—the action which is both judgment within the story and revelation to the reader. It is word, therefore, that is most clearly linked to the meaning of her parables. And the *complete* parable, to amend O'Connor slightly, is "one in which [word] fully illuminates the meaning."[37] The dramatic challenge to the protagonist of the O'Connor story and its effect on the reader are captured perfectly in the eschatological image of the Gospel of John: "Now, you have already been pruned by my words."[38]

2: The Uncollected* Stories

ALTHOUGH "THE GERANIUM" IS AS FAR FROM THE PER-
fection of "Judgement Day" as alpha is from omega, it
gives clear evidence of a strong early inclination toward the
fusion of dramatic narrative and meaning with the hermeneutic function of language. The story is basically
concerned with isolation, or perhaps more accurately,
exile, but whereas "Judgement Day" makes it perfectly
clear that Old Tanner's imagined return to Corinth,
Georgia, is a genuine victory over alienation because he
knows his place, Old Dudley of "The Geranium" remains
exiled from the "true country" of his Southern home. His
isolation, though deserved, seems disproportionately
severe. The reader instinctively knows that what Old
Dudley needs is to return to the freedom of his former
home, even before he remembers his daughter having said,
the day he got sick on the elevated platform, "You'll feel
better when we get home." She is referring of course to
her New York apartment, and Old Dudley, responding
"Home?" apparently realizes the nature of his judgment.
Old Dudley, in fact, never experiences the renewal of a
return to his origins; he is frozen in exile at the end of the
story when, planted in his chair, he replaces the fallen
geranium as a static feature of the tenement window. He
rather than the geranium is now as pathetic as the Grisby
boy at home who "had to be wheeled out every morning
and left in the sun to blink."
Old Dudley is the victim of his daughter's sense of duty
(she would rather have him with her in New York than

21

send him the money he needs to continue at the boarding house), but more importantly he is the victim of his own mistaken sense of place. He is the one who suddenly decided that he wanted to go to New York because "it was an important place"; the decision he lives to regret "wasn't her fault at all." He comes sadly to discover the city's Hadean horrors; its high-rise "dog runs" are built on caves, tunnels, and canals. Everything is "boiling," including people. Like hell, it is literally "nowhere."

The irony of the story is that while Old Dudley has a concern for place, it is woefully misdirected to insignificant things. Although he dislikes the quality of his neighbor's geranium, it nonetheless reminds him of home (where there are "plenty" of "better-looking" ones) and he expects it to be placed on the windowsill across from his at the same time every morning—"about ten." The day of the story, before Old Dudley hears that it has fallen into the alley below, he is annoyed that it has not yet appeared and even more exasperated when he sees the "man in his undershirt" where the geranium is supposed to be. Thus, if the finality of Old Dudley's exile has an adequate motivation in the story, it must be as a judgment leveled against his pervasive superficiality, epitomized by his concern for the proper placement of the geranium rather than his own.

Old Dudley's shallowness pervades even his desire for communication, a motif that undergirds his daughter's thematic statement about "home." No one seems to be able to converse with him to his satisfaction, certainly not his daughter or her family, or for that matter any of the whites in the apartment building. His grandson "was sixteen and couldn't be talked to." When his daughter makes the effort to converse, "first she had to think of something to say." Ironically the only one who voluntarily talks to him is the new tenant—a well-dressed black. But Old Dudley considers this friendliness *out of place*; the black's voice sounds to him "like a nigger's laugh and a white man's sneer." Communication with blacks is in place, as far as Old Dudley is concerned, only when like Rabie back home they know their (inferior) place.

Images of sight and sound appropriately support the thematic concern with displacement and absence of communication, a further confirmation of O'Connor's nascent interest in primordial language. City colors lack the brilliance Old Dudley remembers from his Southern home, and the sounds are discordant. The geranium is such a "pale pink" that it needs "green, paper bows" to liven it up. The sounds of the apartment building include shrill voices, bleating music, crashing cans, slammed doors, and sharp clipped footsteps.

The severity of Old Dudley's alienation is actually an early indication of the significance that O'Connor attached to a proper sense of place. Old Dudley traps himself by his own perversity. Even at home he was prone to entrapment; he had fallen into a hole on a quail hunt because he ignored Rabie's wise advice. When the geranium's owner sarcastically invites Old Dudley to recover the plant from the alley if he wants it, he is unwilling at the last minute to descend the stairs: "He wouldn't go down and have niggers pattin' him on the back." His exile, the unalterable effect of his superficiality, now deepens to self-imposed imprisonment within an apartment in which "there was no place to be where there wasn't somebody else."

An earlier, even less nuanced, version of the story has Old Dudley fall to his death in obvious imitation of the plant itself.

"Why don't you pick up your geranium?" he said.

The man recrossed his arms. "Why don't you, wise guy?"

"I'm gona," Old Dudley murmured.

*   *   *   *

"Flopped like a jelly fish," Mr. Sagelli was telling the little group outside number 10 sixth floor. "Right in front of my eyes. Must have been off his nut."

"He did seem a little queer," a negro in a business suit said. "You know, I talked to him just this morning."

"So what about you!" Mr. Sagelli snorted. "I seen him when he done it."[1]

The published version by contrast ends simply with the expectation of death. He has after all been fighting a tightness in his throat throughout the day—an apprentice's evocation of a stroke in comparison with O'Connor's later masterful handling of George Poker Sash's death. She even allows herself an adolescent double entendre. The geranium has just fallen and Old Dudley is staring at its owner, who seems to be "waiting to see [Old Dudley's] throat pop." In response to Old Dudley's query about why he has not picked up the plant, the man says, "Why don't you, pop?"

The final image of entrapment reveals Old Dudley "framed" by the window he stares through at the man across the way who has told him not to stare. The neighbor has equivalently informed Old Dudley to "mind his own business," a command that the exile is unable to respond to because he had no business being there in the first place. The man's final warning serves to instruct Old Dudley that there are no genuine neighbors in "important places." To leave one's proper place is to choose alienation over communion and death over life. The emblematic geranium, offering a final and somewhat obvious suggestion that Old Dudley will die an exile, lies "at the bottom of the alley with its roots in the air."

"The Barber" is the first of Flannery O'Connor's stories in which her developing preoccupation with words results in their reification. Rayber is a teacher whose pseudo-liberal political preference arouses the traditional bigotry of the barbershop clientele. In supporting the liberal Darmon, Rayber wants, of course, to say the right thing, but in his own defense, not as a mission of conversion to liberalism. When he was first annoyed by the barber's racist treatment of George, the young Negro working for him,

"it was time for [him] to say something but nothing
appropriate would come. He wanted to say something that
George would understand." Rayber not only considers
himself a liberal, he has a condescending fear—not uncommon among teachers—that his language will not be
understood by the masses. As the story develops, we come
to realize that it is not Rayber's superior capacity to
reason or to articulate that constitutes his real problem; he
is pretending to be something he is not and apparently
never will be—a genuine liberal. His inability to communicate on any level follows suit.

Words try to have their effect on Rayber, but he never
really learns. After the first frustrating debate in the
barbershop over Darmon and Hawkson, "the whole asinine
conversation stuck with him the rest of the day and went
through his mind in persistent detail after he was in bed
that night." His response during the day had been
inadequate for lack of preparation, he foolishly permits
himself to think: "To his disgust, he found that he was
going through it, putting in what he would have said if
he'd had an opportunity to prepare himself." The suggestion of his desire to respond by putting on someone else's
attitude—"He wondered how Jacobs would have handled
it"—is a seminal characterization that will mature later in
O'Connor's fiction into the squatting presence of Thomas's
father and the stranger prompting Tarwater. (Jacobs, the
philosopher Rayber admired even though he was not
decisive enough about the racial implications of the
political contest, at least has sense enough to know when
to "argue" with barbers—which is never.) In preparing his
rebuttal for the political showdown, Rayber resolves that
there will be "no waste words, no big words." He tries the
speech out on his wife, and the direction of his eyes
foreshadows the ultimate failure of his words to reach
their mark: "He began saying it very easily and casually,
looking over her head. The sound of his voice playing over
the words was not bad. He wondered if it were the words
themselves or his tones that made them sound the way

they did." His wife, of course, is only feigning attention.

The final encounter with the barbershop mentality is a mock battle between titans of ineptitude. Rayber hears and feels the words leave his mouth as if it had become a rail supporting freight cars: "He heard the words drag out. . . . He felt them pull out of his mouth like freight cars, jangling, backing up on each other, grating to a halt, sliding, clinching back, jarring, and then suddenly stopping as roughly as they had begun." The simile caricatures perfectly Rayber's ridiculous attempt to shore up his own sagging cause through reasoned dialogue.

Jacobs had warned Rayber to leave well enough alone, and his warning is humorously realized in the resolution of the story. Jacob's caution, "Don't spoil your complexion arguing with barbers," becomes Rayber's judgment. As the barber banters with the fat man before Rayber's speech designed to lay ignorance to rest forever, "Rayber reddens." When finally he turns to run from the shop after hitting the barber, "the blood [begins] pounding up Rayber's neck just under the skin." With his half-lathered face and the barber's bib dangling to his knees, Rayber has done more than spoil his complexion; he has lost face completely. His putative wisdom, like lather, melts in the heat of the afternoon sun.

The story does not condemn the liberal position; it condemns the pseudo-liberalism one encounters all too often, a favorite target of O'Connor's later stories. The double entendre of the first sentence of the story tells it all: "It is *trying on* liberals in Dilton" (my emphasis). Rayber is "trying on" liberalism, and the fit is as poor as his final costume. His academic background, rather than strengthening his capacity to reason, has simply turned his prejudice into aggression. The sign that Rayber sees on his final trip to the "peckerwood" barbershop, advertising automatic chicken-killers "So Timid Persons Can Kill Their Own Fowl," is a weak attempt at a hermeneutic pun, implying that Rayber is as "chicken" in hiding his own prejudice behind empty rhetoric as the timid people who need automatic chicken-killers for their fowl. The story does more than intimate that prejudice against ignorance is less tolerable even than prejudice against color.

Although the interpretive role of language in "Wildcat" is muted, one can discern the emergence of a symbolism that supports revelatory communication and will, in the collections especially, become a literary and religious trademark of the author. This is the first of O'Connor's stories in which the presence of the transcendent is patently felt; understanding the experience of God as the *mysterium tremendum* of Rudolf Otto's *Idea of the Holy* is important for an appreciation, not only of the meaning of this story, but also of O'Connor's developing treatment of the subject. Old Gabriel is blind and apparently has been from birth. But his sense of smell is acute, a clear compensation for his lack of sight, and he can of course hear. Nature provides him with vision enough through sound and odor. Yet old Gabriel is not infallible, even if he may have been inclined to think he was until the night of the story's hunt.

Gabriel is old and alone; although the young hunters respect him, they are not above laughter at his expense. Appreciating the keenness of his sense of smell, they want him to tell not only how many of them there are, but also their names. He names three of the four. Even as the story opens then, we know more of Gabriel's margin of error than he has come to realize. His blindness has of course prevented him from ever joining the hunt. There is "gentle mockery" in the Negroes' tone when they ask if he is going with them and, in pointed response to his complaints about their plans for the hunt, when they ask, "How many wildcats you killed, Gabrul?" At the conclusion of the story, when old Gabriel and the hunters still disagree about method, the question is repeated. Neither time is the questioner named. Gabriel's final response—"I knows what I knows, boy"—reflects some of the humility he has learned during the night of waiting, a humility that the probing word itself was designed to instill, clearly beyond the intention of the questioners. Although their taunt prunes Gabriel's pride, it is the smell of the wildcat that speaks more loudly to him than any number of mocking men.

Old Gabriel is sure that the wildcat has returned for more than animal blood. He warns his visitors that the cat is hunter rather than hunted: "It comin' out the woods for mo' than cows. It gonna git itssef some folks' blood. You watch. An' yawl goin' off huntin' it ain't gonna do no good. It goin' huntin' itssef. I been smellin' it." Gabriel recalls how long ago a wildcat killed ol' Hezuh; the story recreates that night from the viewpoint of Gabriel as a blind boy. Evident parallels to the present augment the suspense surrounding old Gabriel's fate. Like ol' Hezuh, he must remain behind with the women while the men go off to hunt. Ol' Hezuh had a woman with him, but she was no protection from the wildcat; old Gabriel is alone.

More than even the wildcat, old Gabriel smells death. His conviction that death is near is as certain as the scent of the wildcat; while precise in his prediction that death would strike the night ol' Hezuh died, he is in error now about its advent because it is his own death he genuinely dreads. Thus when he admits to himself his mistaken estimate of the wildcat's nearness, it is more a wise admission of ignorance about the time of his own death—that uncertainty the Gospels express in terms of our knowing neither the day nor the hour: "He won't sharp like he used to be. They shouldn't leave old people by theyselves." During a night of terror, old Gabriel senses that, though the Lord is waiting on him, "He don't want [him] with [his] face tore open." Yet the proximity of the wildcat so arouses his apprehension of imminent death that he takes the ludicrous precaution of trying to climb on the shelf over the fireplace. Still anxious to hide his fright, he tries later to convince the hunters that the wind tore the shelf loose. Actually, the moment the wildcat struck a half mile away, killing a cow, old Gabriel and the shelf had fallen to the floor.

Old Gabriel is a much chastened man after his lonely passage through the dark night of fear. His realization that he must wait upon the Lord is O'Connor's earliest attempt at expressing what in the person of Mason Tarwater became her most masterful characterization of the prophet's stance of humble expectation in the face of the "threatened intimacy of creation."

"The Crop" is a thoroughly delightful spoof of the pitfalls of the creative writer. What satire there is in the story is so gentle that one is hard pressed to realize that the sterner treatment of similar material in "The Enduring Chill" came from the same author. Rather than employing language hermeneutically in its dramatic structure, "The Crop" is *about* a would-be fiction writer's attempt to use word creatively. Miss Willerton is preoccupied precisely with the power of language. She wants her words to have their best effect, and so she is concerned with the way they *sound*. For instance, the name of the school she attended, Willowpool Female Seminary, "sounded biological" to her and so she "didn't like the phrase." Professedly a great believer in what she calls "phonetic art," she maintains that "the ear [is] as much a reader as the eye." Her talk to the United Daughters of the Colonies had stressed the importance of the "tonal quality ... registered in the ear" for "the success of the literary venture." Equally important apparently is the quality of the "abstract created in the mind" from the picture the eye forms.

"The hardest part of writing a story," she always feels, is deciding what to write about; there are so many possibilities—she thinks! (Ironically, this first and hardest problem she faces proves to be an insurmountable one.) The next, she insists, is getting the story off to a good start. The final difficulty, yet one she does not avert to explicitly, is finishing a story, and the reason Willie never finishes a story seems to lie in her choice of subject matter. Her custom is to begin the process of thinking of an appropriate topic while crumbing the table after meals—

"her particular household accomplishment." But the choice itself is always made before the typewriter, where she can usually do her best thinking. Her principal norm apparently is that the material be "colorful." Bakers, for example, are "hardly colorful enough," nor are teachers. She decides upon sharecroppers, considering the "air of social concern" surrounding their lives to be "valuable to have in the circles she was hoping to travel."

The first sentence, as usual, comes to her "just like a flash": "Lot Motun called his dog." The second sentence presents a problem because both "Lot" and "dog" re-appear, raising the question whether it would be better to have two "dogs" or two "Lots" in the same paragraph. She scratches the second "Lot" for phonetic reasons, deciding that the repetition of the word dog "didn't affect the ears like two 'Lots.' "

When she starts projecting Lot's romantic involvement—"there had to be a woman"—Willie is unable to maintain the requisite distance from her material to keep the creative process in motion. The woman "yowls" and "sneers" at Lot and when a fight ensues Miss Willerton can stand it no longer : "She [strikes] the woman a terrific blow on the head from behind." Her interest in planning "passionate scenes best of all" overwhelms her imagination; it is as if her desire for a "colorful" subject is more an emotional demon than a quality of artistic vision. She replaces Lot's woman, and when the rainy season sets in, she and Lot are expecting both a crop and their first child. Although Lot had wanted a cow instead of a baby, they get neither cow nor the crop—only the baby. As Willie goes into labor, the picture she asks the eye to form is bad abstract expressionism rather than an "abstract" for the mind: "Willie woke in the night conscious of a pain. It was a soft, green pain with purple lights running through it." The rain that has persisted for two days "drones" in Willie's head, as technicolor pain yields to tonal chaos: "Her head rolled from side to side and there were droning shapes grinding boulders in it." Lot is nevertheless pleased with his daughter, insisting that two Willies are "better than a cow, even." When Willie asks Lot what she can do to help him more, she is called back abruptly to the real world by Lucia's answer, "How about your going to the grocery, Willie?" The romantic reverie is over; her creative effort produced no more than an incomplete first paragraph.

As if to prove her basic inability to accept the concrete reality of everyday life that fiction thrives on, Willie is depressed by the grocery because there is "nothing in it but trifling domestic doings." She sees a young couple "walking too close for refinement." The woman is plump and her skin mottled, the man is "long and wasted and shaggy." She *sees*—as he actually is—the Lot she was trying to create; the reality makes her shudder, and she returns home to start on a new topic—one that she probably knows even less about than sharecroppers, the Irish. Their brogue, their history, their spirit will be "more colorful—more arty," she thinks. O'Connor's title ironically predicts that Willie's new subject matter will yield a fictional famine (suggested by "their history") comparable to her other romantic flights from the everyday reality she dislikes. Her imagination will produce a literary crop only when she stops *thinking* while she crumbs the table and starts *observing* the crumbs. Willie's artistic countryside like the crop of the story is not specific enough to become word. The genuinely creative word, the story attests, never misses the trees for the forest.

"The Turkey" even more than "Wildcat" minimizes the dramatic confrontation of language within the limits of human discourse as it explores again the possibilities of hierophany, this time through the developing religious awareness of a young boy. The language that the story deals with therefore is the primordial language of sign, specifically the role of nature as numinous signifier. Whereas the evasive predator in "Wildcat" becomes God's messenger of delayed death to Old Gabriel, the wounded

wild bird in "The Turkey" triggers the child Ruller's first
serious thoughts about God's revelation of Himself to man.

The movement in the story is rhythmic. Ruller, playing
in the woods, spies a wild turkey and while he pursues it
the bird escapes. Resigned, after a fashion, to losing it, he
stumbles upon it again unexpectedly, captures it without
effort (it had been wounded by a hunter), and then loses it
again just as he is about to present the gift to his parents.
The finding-losing-finding-losing rhythm, although cyclic
as a pattern of movement, provokes a youthful theological
response from Ruller that is definitely linear and progres-
sively more profound as he reflects prematurely upon the
experience of the transcendent in the events of his life.

Ruller's deepening sensibility goes from concern for and
reaction against the human word he hears spoken daily to
a response to what he innocently considers to be the divine
word addressed to him through the special event of the
turkey. During the chase, as the wounded turkey flees
through the thicket, Ruller encourages himself by wondering what the words of praise will be like when he returns
with his catch. He imagines the family screaming, "Look at
Ruller with that wild turkey!" Then when he runs into a
tree and momentarily loses his breath, the bird eludes his
grasp for the first time: "It was like somebody had played
a dirty trick on him." The "somebody," he seems to
conclude from the admonitions he has overheard, must be
God. He recalls what his mother and grandmother had
"said" about his older brother's ways and remembers too
"the minister had said young men were going to the devil
by the dozens this day and age." His disappointment, at
any rate, takes the form of a puerile initiation into cursing
and blasphemy. The progression of his offenses goes
from "Nuts" to "Hell" to "God" to "God dammit to
hell" and ultimately to the satisfaction of "God dammit to
hell, good Lord from Jerusalem." He then experiments
with a humorously blasphemous prayer or two, which only
makes him giggle. Finally he seems to realize that he can

best answer God for the loss of the turkey by shocking his grandmother with a few well-chosen profanities.

Just as suddenly as his chase had been interrupted, he discovers "a pile of ruffled bronze with a red head lying limp along the ground." Again he imagines his parents' praise, especially the consoling word that "he's a very unusual child." The reappearance of the bird, now dead from some hunter's bullet, renders his thoughts of God as comically benevolent as only recently they had been impious, at least impish: "Maybe it was to keep him from going bad," he thinks. "Maybe God wanted to keep him from that." Finding the turkey again becomes such an urgent "sign" for Ruller, he wonders whether "maybe God [is] in the bush now, waiting for him to make up his mind." God addresses him, he imagines, as "McFarney," so maturing an experience has His renewed favor been. He feels summoned to declare his goodness by some patent act of charity, and so he plans to give his only dime to some beggar on the way home. So typical is this story of O'Connor's world-in-the-making—where events never work out the way man wants them to—that when Ruller gives his alms to Hetty Gilman (a beggar in fact, but reputed to be wealthy since she has begged so long), "she looked as if she suddenly smelled something bad."

Overwhelmingly disappointing to the boy, however, is the fact that he never reaches home with his prize. It is stolen by an older, and obviously mean, country boy, a "spitter," to whom Ruller is kind enough to show his trophy. When in haste he flees from the country thieves, his fear has overtaken his dejection. God is no longer a child's *mysterium fascinans* but the divine *tremendum* that causes Ruller's premature experience of the agony of loss: "His heart was running as fast as his legs and he was certain that Something Awful was tearing behind him with its arms rigid and its fingers ready to clutch." Instead of the praise he had expected, Ruller is surrounded by an awful silence, word enough to convey a salutary fear of God.

Life gives and it takes away; but dispossession, the story
intimates, is no less a gift than gain.

"The Train," the last of the six stories in the Master's
thesis, affords some interesting structural comparisons
with the preceding five stories; insofar as it was revised and
expanded to become the first chapter in *Wise Blood*, it is
of course materially linked with the following three
stories, all of which eventually found their way into
O'Connor's first novel. While "The Train" is obviously
about death, it avoids the natural symbolism of the
numinous that "Wildcat" employed; taking a human
artifact as symbolic focus for the word, it is closer in
aesthetic inspiration to "The Geranium." Language functions hermeneutically in Mrs. Wallace Ben Hosen's questions to Haze about home, again reminiscent of "The
Geranium"; yet word is more integrally related to meaning
here than in any of the previous stories. The berth-coffin
of "The Train" supports symbolically Mrs. Hosen's queries
and discloses the agony of human limitation, but as a print
whose negative bears traces of mystery.[2]

How the same material is refocused dramatically to fit
the larger setting of *Wise Blood* is better left to our
analysis of the novel. The story deserves to be read as
realized even if difficulty in appreciating its uniqueness
arises from the greater familiarity of the novel. As if to
confirm our earlier suspicion that Willie's practice in "The
Crop" of trying to give a story "the send-off it needed"
reflects O'Connor's habitual concern, the first sentence
emphatically establishes the significance of the berth and
the porter to the meaning of the story. The Pullman berth
in fact is the unifying symbol of the story; what initially is
simply a place to sleep becomes finally a coffin in which
Haze rehearses his death before the porter's detached gaze.
The berth becomes a coffin for Haze precisely because of
the porter. Since the porter must prepare Haze's berth, he
is able to question the black man about his home. Haze is
convinced that the porter is from his own hometown in

Tennessee. He looks enough like old Cash Simmons to be from Eastrod, in fact to be Cash's son, Haze reflects. The porter is actually from Chicago, but because Haze knows that Eastrod is a dying town—"the two families scattered in towns and even the niggers from up and down the road gone into Memphis and Murfreesboro and other places"— he suspects the porter of refusing to acknowledge his humble origins. Haze needs to believe that the porter is from Eastrod to be assured that his past is still somehow alive; the fact that the black man seemingly rejects his home only aggravates Haze's confrontation with mortality.

The significant difference between Hazel Wickers of the story and Haze Motes of the novel is that the latter is consciously fleeing the spiritual residue of his past whereas the former is simply unwilling to accept the passage of time. In the story it is death itself as a physical limit that Haze seems most preoccupied with. The only suggestion the story offers that there may be something beyond death is Haze's wondering whether his mother "walked at night and came there ever (i.e., to their gutted Eastrod house)." He also recalls the unrest that he had seen in her face when she lay in her coffin, "like she wasn't satisfied with resting, like she was going to spring up and shove the lid back and fly out like a spirit going to be satisfied." He had imagined her futile desire to flee when the cover on the coffin was being lowered: "He saw her terrible like a huge bat darting from the closing." Yet we have no indication that these recollections are anything other than Haze's projected unrest—his refusal to accept death.

That the confinement of mortality as well as the fleeting nature of human existence is the thematic center of the story is clear from the pervasive images of enclosure. The berth which becomes Haze's imagined coffin, as we have noted, is mentioned in the opening sentence. The ceiling of the coach is "rounded over him"; it is "low and curved over," but "not quite closed." He "reckons" that they keep the ladder for climbing into the berth "in the closet." Although Haze hopes for a berth with a window so that he can watch the passing countryside, he is disappointed to discover that his berth, like a coffin, has "no window." Finally, he wants the light off so that it will be "all dark." The berth, prepared by the porter who looks like someone from home, triggers Haze's recollection of his last visit home and his discovery of the empty house with only his mother's "walnut shifferrobe" in it. By a process of association he moves in reverie from her "shifferrobe" to her coffin and then is startled to discover himself in a coffin: "From inside he saw it closing, coming closer, closer down and cutting off the light and the room and the trees seen through the window through the crack faster and darker closing down." The sentence is Faulknerian in structure and movement just as the story's theme of death as revealer is plainly related to *As I Lay Dying*.

It is Mrs. Wallace Ben Hosen's question—"Are you going home?—that illumines Haze's problem. Yet the import of the question for the meaning of the story would seem to be fundamentally ironical. When she and Haze, preparing for the night, block each other's way in the aisle, Mrs. Hosen asks with exasperation, "What IS the matter with you?" The deeper implications of this second question had been suggested by the first. Haze's problem is quite simply that he cannot go home because his home no longer exists. He answers cryptically, "It was there," and later, almost pathetically, "It went apart like." Haze had seen the deserted town for the last time during his final furlough before leaving the army; now that he is discharged, he will go instead to Taulkinham where his sister lives. The death of Eastrod has multiple significance for Haze's life. Eastrod represents his past, which, along with his mother and their home, cannot be recreated. Yet Haze apparently will not accept this reminder of man's transitory passage on this earth. Man's life, whether man wants to accept the fact or not, like the train of the story is "grey-flying past instants of trees." Death as passage to one's true home, the theme of *Wise Blood*, is scarcely hinted at here. What O'Connor does capture in the irony of Mrs. Hosen's challenge is the poignancy of man's anticipated death in the inaccessibility of his past.

"The Peeler" is perhaps the most deceptive of the uncollected stories. At first reading it appears diffuse and unstructured. Of the pre-*Wise Blood* stories it seems least capable of independent existence; indeed, it undergoes only minor changes in translation into the third chapter of the novel. Yet a closer look reveals a fairly complex and unique story that, far from perfect, nonetheless blends episodic structure and interrupted dialogue into a dramatically plausible whole.

The title itself provides an adequate entrance to the meaning of the story. On the literal level, it is the peeler of course that serves to bring the principal characters together—Haze Motes, Enoch Emery, and Asa Shrike and his daughter. Each watches the potato-peeling demonstration for his own purpose. Enoch is lonely and hopes to make some meaningful human contact. Asa Shrike is a proselytizing pentecostal anxious to capitalize on the presence of any crowd. Haze is drifting through the evening streets of Taulkinham, not at all sure what he is looking for but looking "as if he were trying to smell something that was always being drawn away." This revealing simile is the story's initial indication that Haze's restlessness is more compulsion than aimless drifting.

On a deeper level the peeler serves to emphasize the fact that another kind of peeling has been, is, and will perhaps continue to be a significant part of the lives of the principal characters. The story humorously relates the peeling of potatoes to human nudity. As the focus of attention shifts from object to subject, peeling becomes undressing and the latter is an evident metaphor for concupiscence. The only way that Enoch Emery was able to escape from the woman who had traded for him with his father was to go into "her room without [his] pants on and [pull] the sheet off her and giver a heart attackt." Asa Shrike's daughter, not yet the completely promiscuous

Sabbath Lily of *Wise Blood*, is nonetheless trying to seduce Haze and Enoch. In fact, Haze claims that he follows Asa and his daughter to give her the peeler he bought in order to prove that he "ain't beholden for none of her fast eye like she gave [him] back yonder." Later she gives the peeler to Enoch and asks him to visit her. When Haze returns to Leora Watts's, she knows immediately why he is back: "She sat up and pulled her nightgown from under her and took it off." More inhibited, Haze undresses in the dark.

The story's conclusion shifts abruptly from the present at Leora's house to the past of Haze's youth and his first experience of sexual exhibitionism at a carnival. Seeing the nude woman there, squirming in the coffin to the utter delight of the lecherous men gathered around her, the young Haze had made sin's acquaintance and felt the need of repentance for the first time. His mother, dressed in the black that she always wore, knew that her twelve-year-old son had somehow been exposed to evil. This episode from Haze's youth, unlike the later experience with Leora Watts, occasions more than a struggle with the guilt of actual sin. Under his mother's reproving gaze, Haze "forgot the guilt of the tent for the nameless unplaced guilt that was in him." This "nameless unplaced guilt" that Haze tries to atone for is man's perennial experience of the attractiveness of sin, the innate inclination to evil resulting from original sin. It is this sinful condition common to men, the concupiscence symbolized by the peeler, that Haze seems unwilling to accept. More by far than a parable about human carnality, the story is fundamentally concerned with Haze's struggle against the realization that man is incomplete. Both action and dialogue blend dramatically and structurally to serve this theme of man's radical poverty. "The Peeler" is Flannery O'Connor's most explicit, if not her most subtle, story about original sin.

Isolation is integral to our understanding of original sin; aloneness is perhaps man's typical psychological experience of his unfinished nature. Moreover, a customary expression of the Christian mystery of redemption views the power of Christ as curative; in religious terminology, man lives with the possibility of growth toward wholeness. Grace heals the division *within* man (concupiscence warring against reason) and *among* men. Language functions interpretively in the story to illumine Haze's isolation as well as his need for healing. Countering Haze's argument against the purchase of a peeler on the grounds that he has no one at home, the salesman rejoins for the sake of the people, "Well, shaw . . . he needs one theseyer just to keep him company." Despite the obvious humor of Haze's needing a machine for company, the statement accentuates Haze's isolation as well as the mechanism implied in his denial of spirit. Enoch's word of judgment is far more serious, in view of his own extreme loneliness, when he compares Haze's unfriendliness to the coldness of urban indifference: "People ain't friendly here. You ain't from here and you ain't friendly either."

Whereas Enoch and the salesman illumine the negative side of the human condition, Asa Shrike in a typical pentecostal broadside assures Haze that he knows the real reason why he has followed them. "You're marked," he asserts. And, again, "I can hear the urge for Jesus in your voice." The "secret need" that Asa insists Haze has is to accept the possibility of being healed. The chief distress of the human condition, the story proposes, is man's unwillingness to admit the inner demand for healing that transcends his own refusal to hope. Haze like all other men yearns to be made whole.

Aside from the supportive role of the story's dialogue, both the episodic structure of the narrative and the abrupt shift in temporal sequence at the end of the story corroborate its thematic concern with original sin. Form in "The Peeler" is quite clearly meaning. The narrative is purposefully episodic. If no single encounter appears complete, the interruptions simply magnify the incompleteness Haze experiences within himself. The salesman's attempt to keep the attention of the crowd is broken by

Shrike's distribution of pentecostal tracts. Haze disrupts
the proselytizing venture when he shreds the leaflet Asa
has given him. Enoch punctuates Haze's attentive pursuit
of the evangelist with the story of his life. In front of the
auditorium Haze again interrupts Shrike's missionary
efforts. Enoch's overtures of friendship are rudely terminated by Haze's return to Leora Watts. And the final
sequence of the narrative in present time is broken when
Haze's undressing becomes, by auctorial fiat, a re-creation
of his first exposure to concupiscence through nudity.
This abrupt shift in temporal perspective not only confirms the pattern of disruption that signifies human
limitation, but also serves to place the origin of Haze's
problem where it genuinely belongs—in his past—just as
Genesis locates the beginning of human imperfection at
the dawn of the race. Appropriately, the story ends where
man's problem begins.

The boy Haze had experienced no consoling sign from
God in response to the penance he did; he nevertheless
tried to atone. The ultimate irony of the story seems to be
that Haze the young man, although reluctant to accept his
unfinished nature and even consciously denying the
existence of sin, may be closer to a healing realization. The
force that draws him is powerful enough to make him
"clean"; it will continue to elude him and us, though, until
we accept our human birthmark.

"The Heart of the Park" follows "The Peeler" in Robert
Giroux's arrangement of *The Complete Stories*, but it is
not because the latter was published first (his general norm
for sequence). Both stories appeared for the first time in
1949 in the *Partisan Review* (volume 16), "The Heart of
the Park" in the February issue and "The Peeler" in
December. Giroux places "The Peeler" first because this
was the order in which the stories were incorporated into
Wise Blood.

Even though "The Heart of the Park" seems to
presuppose the events of "The Peeler," certain internal

evidence suggests that "The Peeler" was indeed written after "The Heart of the Park"—a high probability considering the jigsaw pattern O'Connor appears to have followed in piecing the novel together.[3] In "The Heart of the Park," Haze is Mr. Hazel Weaver and Asa's last name is Moats (a slightly different spelling of the one that eventually becomes Haze's). The Haze of "The Peeler," however, is closer to the Haze of the novel: he has the same last name and he insists on his cleanness. He assures Shrike, "Listen, . . . I'm as clean as you are." Thus, when "The Heart of the Park" was rewritten as chapter 5 of the novel, Hazel Weaver's "I ain't clean" becomes Haze Motes's more characteristic "I AM clean."

One of the problems with considering "The Heart of the Park" apart from its setting in the *Wise Blood* cycle is that it appears structurally to be Enoch Emery's story. Its highly controlled patterns all tend to indicate that Enoch's characterization is of central importance. And if the only dramatic tension of any interest stems from Haze's appearance and his reluctant initiation into the mysteries of "the dark secret center of the park," we know too little about him. We never find out, for instance, precisely why Haze wants to see "those people named Moats." We know only that his need is urgent and that it is somehow related to his obsession with uncleanness.

There is nevertheless sufficient evidence for considering "The Heart of the Park" Haze's story rather than Enoch's. The role of active response to the story's conflict is really Haze's, for even if Enoch gives the appearance of acting while showing Haze his secret, he is decidedly a passive figure. His inability to rise above an animal level of existence is so pronounced that he is finally little more than part of the natural setting. Haze alone is developed enough spiritually to be able to react on a personal level to the revelation of the mystery.

Enoch is the agent of that revelation. His "wise blood" had been telling him all morning that "the person would come today"; so when Haze drives up to the pool where

Enoch begins his daily ritual, he knows that Haze is the chosen initiate and that when he sees the secret at the heart of the park, "something's going to happen." For Enoch, the glass case contains "a mystery" despite the fact that its contents are plainly there for everyone to see. What the typewritten card on front did not say was "inside him, a terrible knowledge without any words to it, a terrible knowledge like a big nerve growing inside him." Enoch is unable to articulate the meaning of his secret, not because it represents ineffable mystery, but simply because he is less than fully human. The simile used to characterize his knowledge—"a big nerve growing inside him"—verifies our impression that his response remains on an instinctual level. Moreover, his faculty of speech is not connected with the other function of his brain, which is "figuring," not "thinking": "Enoch's brain was divided into two parts. The part in communication with his blood did the figuring but it never said anything in words. The other part was stocked with all kinds of words and phrases." Whereas the Enoch of the novel (and of "Enoch and the Gorilla") definitely regresses from the subhuman to the status of a higher ape, Enoch in "The Heart of the Park" functions exclusively as a human *animal.*

Enoch's approach to the park's mystery is compulsively in three stages. Going to the swimming pool, to the FROSTY BOTTLE, and to the zoo have become such a "very formal and necessary" preparation for his visit to the Museum that he will not take Haze there until he too has passed through the initiatory stages. Although the preparations parody ritual and the museum is described as if it were a religious shrine, there is nothing consciously religious about the process or the mystery for Enoch; it is little more than superstitious incantation.[4]

The significance of the ritual gradually dawns upon Haze, although he, like the reader, must wait for the final revelation to understand the connection between initiation and mystery. What develops is an awareness that man's concupiscence of the flesh is linked to his recent emergence from the animal kingdom and that both concupiscence and man's manifest animal vestiges are signs of his radical incompleteness and mortality. And it is not the spoken word that is the medium of this message but rather the language of the eyes. The centrality of vision is emphasized by Enoch's comic mispronunciation of the Classical Latin spelling of the word M V S E V M over the entrance to his shrine: "He pointed down through the trees. 'Muvseevum,' he said. The strange word made him shiver" (my emphasis).

At each of the three ritual stages, man's bond with the beast is illumined in action and/or image. The reason why Enoch first hides in the abelia bushes near the pool is to watch the women swimming and sunning. Voyeurism is a pathological human variation on an animal urge. He likes particularly the splits in the sides of the women's suits and the way they bare their shoulders for sunning. When Haze arrives, Enoch, like an animal on the prowl, appears "on all fours at the end of the abelia." The woman with two boys pulls "the bathing suit straps off her shoulders," and Enoch whispers, "King Jesus." ("King Kong" would more suitably express his basic allegiance.) The combination of exposure and blasphemy sends Haze bolting back to his car. As he and Enoch ride away, Haze's face is "sour and froglike."

Enoch's second stop is at the FROSTY BOTTLE, where drinking a daily milkshake is nothing more than a front for making "a few suggestive remarks to the waitress whom he believes to be secretly in love with him." Haze is too preoccupied to order, and Enoch tells the waitress, "He ain't hungry but for just to see you." This second phase of Enoch's ritual links two physiological activities man shares with the animals, eating and sex. The images continue to associate man and animal. An advertisement for ice cream shows "a cow dressed like a housewife." And Haze's withdrawn appearance suggests a turtle in hiding; he stands stiffly in the middle of the room, "his neck drawn down inside his collar."

The first two phases of Enoch's ritual emphasize the beast in man by using animal imagery to describe humans. The final step, his visit to the zoo, emphasizes the animality of man by the ironic use of human imagery for describing animals. The two black bears that Enoch and Haze see are "like two matrons having tea, their faces polite and self-absorbed." Enoch scorns the animals, no doubt because his "wise blood" secretly resents its kinship with them: "Usually he stopped at every cage and made an obscene comment aloud to himself." The animals return the favor, but in human form: "Every animal there had a personal haughty hatred for him like society people have for climbers." At the pool and the FROSTY BOTTLE humans looked at other humans with animal intentions. Now the process is reversed to match the inversion of the imagery; animals regard humans with human, if not divine, intentions. A hoot owl, like a self-sustaining eye in the middle of a mop, "was looking directly at Hazel Weaver." Just as he had said to the waitress at the FROSTY BOTTLE, Haze says to the eye, "I ain't clean," as if fully accepting the silent judgment from the cage. The uncleanness Haze senses is of an order of awareness essentially superior to Enoch's preoccupation with the refuse in the cages.

In addition to the human and animal parallels at each of the three stages, the imagery of the first and last stages viewed in relationship to the mystery itself suggests successive phases of the evolutionary process. The woman in the pool looks like an amphibian leaving the water: "She rose on her hands until a large foot and leg came up from behind her and another on the other side and she was out, squatting there, panting." In the zoo sequence, the narrative progresses to the level of man's predecessor, the ape; finally, in the glass case at the heart of the park we have the crown of the process, man himself—but naked, shrunken, and dead. Haze is absorbed in this vision of death, his eyes riveted on the mummy. With characteristic humor O'Connor imagines the instructive humility that she undoubtedly feels the head of the line should possess: "[The mummy's] eyes were squinched shut as if a giant block of steel were falling down on top of him." Haze's own eyes seem "like two clean bullet holes" in the glass top of the case. But the moment of silent revelation is broken when the woman with the two boys appears; her grinning face is concupiscence itself reflected in the glass over Haze's. She is even less capable of appreciating the significance of the secret than Enoch; he at least possesses a certain instinctual awe.

The intensity of Haze's reaction to the recurring specter of uncleanness indicates perhaps the frightening proximity of his grace of self-acceptance. His desire to locate the preacher is frustrated by Enoch's determination to share the secret of the park with him. He leaves in panic without the address, although he makes one last futile attempt to get it when Enoch pursues him. He has no doubt come closer to spiritual realization in the heart of the park, where he did not expect to find it, than he would have at the preacher's house where he sought it. Enoch offers mysterious knowledge he can never fathom. To prevent that revelation from overtaking himself, Haze fells Enoch violently with a rock. Enoch sits stunned in the center of the park, in the heart of the city, taking animal delight in the drops of his "wise blood" that have fallen to the ground.

Thematically the story is a linear development from the two previous stories. "The Train" considers the limit that death imposes on human existence; "The Peeler," probing more deeply into the human condition, investigates concupiscence as a sign of human limitation. "The Heart of the Park" places the roots of human limitation—both mortality and concupiscence—in man's link with the animal kingdom. The waitress at the FROSTY BOTTLE anticipates the full redemptive possibility in the "squinched" eyes of the mummy at the heart of the park when she calls Haze "clean," claiming "there ain't anything sweeter than a clean boy," but Haze's response—"I

ain't clean"—is far closer to the point of the story.
Accepting the mystery of man's humble origin and his
developing nature is indeed a first but major threshold one
must cross to become "clean." Haze has spirit enough to
perceive the radical limits of man's flesh, yet he is still
unwilling to accept in himself the consequences of that
mysterious union of spirit and flesh. If the story fails to be
explicit about the dimensions of spirit, it is pellucid about
Haze's weakening denial of his tainted flesh.

"Enoch and the Gorilla," the last of the four stories in
the *Wise Blood* cycle, represents a perfect counterpoint to
whatever progress toward self-acceptance Haze has made.
Although it is manifestly Enoch's story, it is simul-
taneously an indictment of man's city. Enoch, who in
"The Heart of the Park" scorned the animals he visited
every day in the zoo, discovers that the public has been
invited to shake the hand of Gonga, "Giant Jungle
Monarch and a Great Star." The promotional gimmick for
the jungle movie seems tailored to Enoch's aversion: "To
his mind, an opportunity to insult a successful ape came
from the hand of Providence." Typically it develops into
another situation in which Enoch is tricked by Fate.
O'Connor chooses her vocabulary carefully in making the
distinction between Providence and Fate. Enoch mistakenly "figures" that he is free to control his encounter
with the ape (Providence mysteriously governs the *free*
actions of men); Fate actually controls his life inasmuch as
he lacks any genuine freedom. Enoch experiences the
inexorable result of the conflict between his obsession and
urban inhumanity.

"Roaring Gonga" is a total fraud; he is certainly no star.
O'Connor's satiric view of movie promotion that reaches
perfection in George Poker Sash's Confederate dance with
death capitalizes here on the utter hypocrisy of "art" as
business. Gonga's prima donna antics exasperate his
co-workers to the point of blasphemy. He refuses to leave
the wagon until he is able to protect his costume and

himself from the rain: "A dark furry arm emerged just enough for the rain to touch it and then drew back inside. 'Goddamn,' the man who was under the marquee said; he took off his raincoat and threw it to the man by the door, who threw it into the wagon. After two or three minutes more, the gorilla appeared at the door, with the raincoat buttoned up to his chin and the collar turned up." Throughout his ordeal of shaking hands with his human fans—the first ten brave enough to step up are being admitted to the movie free—Gonga has a hard time concealing his boredom: "The gorilla kept his hand extended and turned his head away with a bored look at the rain."

The imminent opportunity to make "an obscene remark that would be suitable to insult [Gonga] with" seems to paralyze Enoch's brain. "Both parts" are now "completely empty." The "warm and soft" feeling of "the first hand that had been extended to Enoch since he had come to the city" melts his scorn into comical submission. With the simplicity of a child approaching Santa Claus, Enoch mumbles a feeble introduction: "My name is Enoch Emery. . . . I attended the Rodemill Boy's Bible Academy. I work at the city zoo. I seen two of your pictures. I'm only eighteen years old but I already work for the city. My daddy made me come. . . ." Just as a surly voice inside the ape-suit says, "You go to hell," the "star's" hand jerks away. If Enoch had not distracted himself with thoughts about "Providence"—clearly beyond his range for "figuring"—he could have realized perhaps when he was reading the advertisement that "Fate [had begun] drawing back her leg to kick him."

Despite the embarrassment, Enoch persists in "the expectation that something [is] going to happen to him." Armed with his landlady's umbrella, denuded so that all that "was left was a black stick with a sharp steel point at one end and a dog's head at the other," he begins an evening of violent discovery. Earlier he had considered the delapidated umbrella to be "at least as old as [the landlady] was." It signifies in fact more primitive times. As the evening unfolds, it is both phallus when he prods the hip of the waitress and perhistoric tool as he digs the hole to bury his human costume, after wresting from Gonga a more appropriate vesture. Stripped, the umbrella "might have been an instrument of some specialized torture that had gone out of fashion." In Enoch's hands, and with Fate's direction, the umbrella becomes Neanderthal weapon.

Enoch senses that the evening will further his ambition "to better his condition." His nervousness arises from a premonition that the honor he is setting off to get may have to be snatched rather than received. "The virtue of hope, in Enoch," we are told, "[is] made up of two parts of suspicion and one part lust." So when the newspaper borrowed from the customer at the Paris Diner announces that Gonga will make his last appearance in the city that night at the Victory(!) Theater, Enoch's countenance is transformed. The waitress takes his "look of awakening" to be an indication that he has swallowed a seed. From there Enoch's rise to "stardom" is deceptively smooth. Hiding in Gonga's van, he subdues his idol and seizes the gorilla costume (the extent of his own scars would suggest his victim is dead as well as vanquished). Transformation becomes deformation as Enoch in Gonga's clothing reverts to pure animal. In a bit of self-conscious commentary on the narrative the author assures us that "burying his clothes was not a symbol to him of burying his former self." Enoch the Gorilla is no new creation; it is an honest retreat behind a threshold he cannot claim.

As he begins "to growl and beat his chest," the object of his ambition is paradoxically clear. Wearing Gonga's suit will afford him the minimal human contact he has sought. Yet the imaginary hand that he clutches in practice is as close as he will ever come to the reality of human communication. "The figure extended its hand, clutched nothing, and shook its arm vigorously; it withdrew the arm, extended it again, clutched nothing, and shook." The first people he approaches with extended hand, a couple sitting on a rock "looking across an open stretch of valley at a view of the city in the distance," are evidently the last he ever sees. Their flight leaves him temporarily etched against the "uneven skyline of the city" he cannot penetrate. As pitiable as it seems, his return to the woods is more honest than the continued occupation of the city by dehumanized "stars." Enoch at least is where he belongs. His progressive alienation from the city of man, the story seems to say, is due just as much to the depersonalization of the city as it is to Enoch's inability to transcend his animal nature. Western man's characteristic gesture of greeting, the handshake, becomes the story's ironic metaphor for the absence of communication. The story abounds in tactile references, but no character ever truly touches another. The reason is obvious: there are no genuine humans in the story. Contact shielded by the gorilla costume and distanced by Enoch's umbrella shaft typifies the alienation of impersonal existence. If "Enoch and the Gorilla" is O'Connor's severest parody of the human condition, there is at least a playful tone to her image of the city as zoo.

"You Can't Be Any Poorer Than Dead," published in 1955, reappeared in an expanded and revised form five years later as the opening chapter of *The Violent Bear It Away*. The transformations that the material underwent reaffirm the structural simplicity of the short story form in comparison with the novel. In "You Can't Be Any Poorer Than Dead," the conflict between Mason and Tarwater is kept in the starkest relief; descriptive elements that were later amplified to give the novel its grotesque breadth and religious complexity are often only suggested in the short story and usually merely humorous in effect. The Powder-head of the novel is a nameless clearing, and Bishop is simply Rayber's "son"—a fat, bespectacled boy, not the idiot child he becomes. In fact, the only time that Mason brings Tarwater to the schoolteacher's house, Mason is the one who acts most peculiarly, "staring at the little boy and rolling his tongue around outside his mouth like an old idiot." It is perhaps nothing more than a friendly gimmick to get the child's attention.

The dramatic conflict of the short story arises from Mason's desire for full Christian burial; this is of course a factor in the novel, but it is no more than a preliminary stage in Tarwater's attempted rejection of the imposed prophetic mission to baptize Bishop. Mason conceives the requested burial as the least he can ask of Tarwater in return for saving him "from that ass in town." "Now all I'm asking in return," Mason insists, "is when I die to get me in the ground where the dead belong and set up a cross over me to show I'm there. That's all in the world I'm asking you to do." Tarwater protests that he will be "too wore out" for "trifles" like crosses. In language that is certainly atypical of O'Connor's fictional world—but then Mason *is* different from any of her other key characterizations—he responds: "You'll learn what a trifle is on the day those crosses are gathered! Burying the dead right may be the only honor you ever do yourself." It is the bald affirmation of self-realization through fraternal concern that is so surprising.

As in the novel, Tarwater permits the stranger whose voice he hears and cannot initially distinguish from his own (and, little wonder, since he is no stranger to Tarwater at all, but his own unbridled inclinations) to convince him that fire would be much easier than burial as a way of disposing of the "bull-like old man." Against Mason's belief that "the world was made for the dead," considering "all the dead there are"—"there's a million times more dead than living and the dead are dead a million times longer than the living are alive!"—Tarwater develops the philosophy, born of laziness and license, that "you can't be any poorer than dead." As in the *Wise Blood* stories, mortality is the most radical sign of man's poverty, but here the tone is more obviously humorous. The saying originates "in the voice of the stranger." Anticipating death and being dead differ the way sign and reality do; being dead is therefore as poor as one can be, Tarwater's "voice" concludes. Being left to the mercy of the likes of his stranger is indeed destitution of the worst sort. Thus the story takes exception to the stranger's slogan when it suggests finally that one *can* be poorer than dead: one can be alive without meaning, or, worse still, with perverted purpose.

The options presented to Tarwater are basically the same in the short story as in the novel, the minor exceptions being that in the short story the voices of perverted meaning are necessarily fewer and Tarwater's "stranger" is incarnated in the unnamed copper flue salesman (Meeks in the novel). The stranger and the salesman both have "sharp" faces and wear "stiff broad-brimmed" hats. In the novel O'Connor makes the stranger's hat a "panama," which links his definitive incarnation more clearly to the homosexual rapist, while retaining the suggestion that Meeks is the first in a line of spiritual confidence men rivaling Melville's.[5] In the short story, the stranger and the salesman actively oppose the option urged by Mason and Buford. It is no doubt significant that the former go unnamed: they represent a world without obligation, love, or mystery. The latter, both named, offer one of discipline, concern, and awe.

If the words of the stranger and the salesman are not enough to specify the diabolical origin of their opinions, related demonic imagery confirms our reading. This is true also of Rayber whose negative influence in the story is pronounced even though he is present to its action only in memory. After Mason had shot him in the leg, the schoolteacher, departing in haste from the Edenic clearing, made "a disappearing rattle in the corn." When Tarwater starts drinking at his great-uncle's still, the imagery describing the effect of the liquor is directly related to the stranger's preceding counsel: "A burning arm slid down Tarwater's throat as if the devil were already reaching inside him to finger his soul." A Dantean atmosphere of infernal darkness engulfs the salesman's and Tarwater's midnight ride toward the city down "the black untwisting highway." The glow of the distant city that Tarwater confuses with his burning conscience left at the clearing is by implication the fire of Dis, where self-identity is lost in the torture of urban anonymity. For it was while Mason was living in the city with the "Peeping Tom" that he became a specimen of "extinct" religious man in Rayber's psychological monograph; and Tarwater's hat, the symbol of his selfhood, had fallen twelve stories "into the pit of the city street."

It is Buford, whose presence is an extension of the old man's dominance, who utters the story's warning. When he finds Tarwater drunk at the still, he reminds him that his great-uncle "needs to be rested"—a service we know from the masterful opening sentence that Buford must return to perform. Before leaving him to his drunken sleep, the Negro mutters, "Nobody going to bother you. . . . That going to be your trouble." The judgment he announces comes at that moment of quiet climax in the story between the inner victory of the permissive "stranger" and his demonic incarnation in the double-talking salesman hawking love without meaning. Unlike his avatar in the novel, this earlier Tarwater, whose attempted cremation of his great-uncle's body destroys his only worthwhile home, flees finally into the merited hell of a world where "nobody [owes] nobody nothing." If the word addressed to us does not "bother" us, the story states precisely, it is not authentic human language. Nor is it grace in *any* sense.

In "The Partridge Festival," the protagonist, Calhoun, has come home for the "tribal rites" of the annual azalea festival, mainly because the nonconformist Singleton had added some unexpected excitement to the festivities. Tried by a mock court for refusing to buy a festival badge and imprisoned with a goat previously convicted of the same offense, Singleton responded by killing six people—five festival dignitaries and a bystander. Singleton's picture had captured Calhoun's imagination; he thought he saw in it "the composure of the man . . . who is willing to suffer for the right to be himself." Calhoun allows himself not only to note a certain physical resemblance to his rebel-martyr, but also—more significantly—to postulate a deep inner bond: "Though his eyes were not mismatched, the shape of his face was broad like Singleton's; but the real likeness between them was interior." Ostensibly Calhoun wants to write a novel that will vindicate the reputed madman. "Singleton was only the instrument," he insists, "Partridge itself is guilty." The novel will "show, not say" how primary injustice operates, how Partridge needs a scapegoat to expiate its sins of commercialism and hypocrisy. Calhoun considers conducting a street discussion in the Socratic method, but as he surveys the scene he sees no one who looks "capable of any genuine interest in meaning."

He lives, moreover, with the perpetual embarrassment that it was his grandfather, "the master merchant," who had given Partridge its motto: "Beauty is Our Money Crop." Actually, Calhoun hopes to mitigate the guilt of his own materialism. He spends his summers selling "air-conditioners, boats, and refrigerators so that for the other nine months he [can] afford to meet life naturally and bring his real self—the rebel-artist-mystic—to birth," which means simply that he spends the rest of the year doing nothing.

His great-aunts arrange a date for him with their neighbor Mary Elizabeth, who is home from college for the spring holidays. Two peas in a pod, they clearly deserve each other's company. Mary Elizabeth shares Calhoun's estimate of the people of Partridge: "They prostitute azaleas!" she says. She intends to write a nonfiction study proving Singleton a Christ-figure—of course, "as myth." Although Calhoun can see that Mary Elizabeth will soon "turn into a full-grown ogre—false intellect, false emotions, maximum efficiency, all operating to produce the dominant hair-splitting Ph.D.," he persuades her that they

should have "an existential encounter" with Singleton.
The novelist is interested in the mystery of personality,
and the sight of Singleton may possibly enrich Mary
Elizabeth's theories. Calhoun has the secret but prophetic
hope that the sight of Singleton suffering may "raise him
once and for all from his commercial instincts."

They feign kinship with Singleton to gain admittance
into the prison; their kinship with him and with each other
is, in fact, more real than imaginary. As they sit waiting for
Singleton to be brought in, they are fused in single
anticipation of catastrophe: "The two sat together as if
they were waiting for some momentous event in their
lives—a marriage or instantaneous deaths. They seemed
already joined in a predestined convergence." They have
come to look at Singleton, but what they see is themselves,
the revelation of their own ugly hypocrisy. Singleton goes
berserk at the chance to proposition Mary Elizabeth; and
when he begins to pull his hospital gown over his head,
screaming, "Look girl!" they see the nakedness of their
complicity and flee in panic to the safety of Calhoun's car
and the open road. In a wedding of self-realization, each
looks into the other's eyes and sees the mote in his own.

How O'Connor's art, specifically her use of imagery,
developed in support of the interpretive word of revelation
is evident when we compare the published version of the
story with an earlier complete version entitled "The
Partridge Pageant." The beginning and the end of the
earlier version follow. The framing references to the
festival flags—absent from the published version—are necessary for discerning the effect of the experience on
Calhoun. The concluding two paragraphs below corres-
pond to the last paragraph of the final version; they follow
Singleton's climactic act of exhibitionism.

A red and gold banner that said PARTRIDGE
BICENTENNIAL flapped against the upper girders of
the river bridge. The boy was not shocked that it
remained up and that everything was going on as

usual. . . . Not one banner or flag had been taken down. Partridge would bury its dead but would not lose a nickel.

* * * *

Mary Elizabeth was already dashing out the room and the boy ran behind her and thrust open the glass entrance door just in time to prevent her running into it. They scrambled into the car and drove away with nothing in their heads but the instinct to be gone. When they were well away from the place, he stopped the car on the side of the road and they turned to face one another as if sooner or later it had to be done, but after one glance, each turned away. It was as if neither knew how to hide what now appeared shameful.

In a moment the boy felt that he could look again. He looked and blinked as if his vision had suffered a readjustment. He perceived strange depths about him, strange hollows in the girl's eyes, strange gaps in the woods behind her. The world was altered. He looked down the narrowing highway. He felt that the road to Partridge must have lengthened and that when they reached it, they would find that the place itself had somehow changed its shape. He had a moment of revulsion, then he felt a return of his ecstatic sadness and had a vision of all the little flags of Partridge, mysteriously flying.[6]

Whatever effect the revelation in this earlier version has on Calhoun and Mary Elizabeth is muted at best. As in the final version Singleton's "Look girl!" exposes their hypocritical lives, but here judgment falls short of response. Calhoun and Mary Elizabeth, like the flags of Partridge, remain basically unaffected. Calhoun's "moment of revulsion" passes; his normal mood of "ecstatic sadness" returns. In the published version, however, there is no missing the effect of Singleton's words, the acceptance of revelation. Singleton's nakedness becomes cosmic revela-

tion. As they drive away in panic, "the sky [is] *bone-white*
and the slick highway [stretches] before them like a piece
of the earth's *exposed nerve*." And Mary Elizabeth's face
"[seems] to mirror the *nakedness* of the sky" (my
emphases). These added images strengthen the hermeneutic function of language in the story.

Calhoun is transfixed by the vision of his own hypocrisy
as he gazes at the image of his great-grandfather in Mary
Elizabeth's glasses. From early in the story the reader at
least has been prepared to accept this recognition of their
spiritual affinity. Part of his great-aunts' ritual each time
Calhoun visits is to show him a miniature portrait of his
great-grandfather, as if their understanding of the spiritual
legacy definitely exceeds his own. The old man is
"round-faced, bald, and altogether unremarkable-looking;
...his expression [is] all innocence and determination."
Later, in the barbershop, the image that confronts Calhoun
in the mirror is "round-faced, unremarkable-looking and
innocent." Reacting unconsciously to a baleful revelation,
he talks "belligerently" to the barber and his expression
turns "fierce." Thus, when he is startled by the "miniature
visage" in Mary Elizabeth's spectacles, he is at last able to
acknowledge the image in which he was made: "Round,
innocent, undistinguished as an iron link, it was the face
whose gift of life had pushed straight forward to the future
to raise festival after festival. Like a master salesman, it
seemed to have been waiting there from all time to claim
him." The city of Partridge is condemned along with
Calhoun and Mary Elizabeth; there is a universal brotherhood in crass materialism. Partridge was right about
Singleton's insanity, but it was in no position either to cast
the first stone.

The last of the previously uncollected stories, "Why Do
the Heathen Rage?" was originally published just a year
before O'Connor's death as an "excerpt from the beginning sections" of her "as yet untitled" third novel.[7] The

excerpt, however, stands in its own right as a short story and was certainly considered as such by Robert Giroux when he collected *The Complete Stories*. On the basis of the four characters presented in the tale—Tilman, his wife, and their two children, Walter and Mary Maud—it is by no means certain who the principal character of the novel was going to be, although a strong assumption would favor Walter. The story as it stands is the mother's; it is designed to answer—in her disfavor—the question of its title. The heathens rage because they try, contrary to Jesus' warning (Matt. 6:24), to serve two masters, God *and* mammon, and as a result serve only the latter well.

Although the New Testament saying of Jesus indicates precisely the options that the story illustrates, the question of the title and the answer supported by O'Connor's story come from Psalm 2 in the Old Testament. In the Authorized King James Version, the psalmist's query is "Why do the heathen rage, and the people imagine a vain thing?" The psalm is not one that is explicitly attributed to David, yet its sentiments and personal references are indisputably Davidic. The heathens conspire because the Lord has made David king and given him the nations as his heritage. The kings of the earth plot in vain: they take counsel against the all-powerful Lord of the universe. David for his part advocates wisdom and holy fear; God's wrath, he warns, is quickly kindled. O'Connor's heathens rage in vain since they have chosen the wrong master.

Both Tilman and his wife are described in terms of rage. Tilman has had a stroke while on business in the state capital, and on the day that he returns home by ambulance—the occasion of the story—the only part of his face that is not "prepared for death" is his left eye: "Twisted inward, [it] seemed to harbor his former personality. It burned with rage." When the stretcher carrying Tilman passes Walter, his fascinated but unmoved son, Tilman's "enraged left eye appeared to include him in its vision but he gave him no sign of recognition." The lack of recognition confirms Walter's role as antagonist in this brief drama about the abandonment of an enraged, rapacious older generation.

For Tilman, justice has already struck. His wife, weaker partner to the cult of mammon, yet possessing her own proportionate fury, feels inadequate to assume control of the family and management of its affairs. It is her frenzied hope that the tragedy incapacitating Tilman will "wake Walter up." When she tells Walter "the responsibility is [his] now," her face is "hard," her posture is "rigid," and she speaks "in a harsh, final voice." And as she reads from Walter's book that "love should be full of anger," she admits to herself that she is "furious all the time." She regrets Walter's inability to rise to the challenge; in vain she searches "for some sign in his big bland face that some sense of urgency had touched him, some sense that now he had to take hold, that now he had to do something, anything." To her mind even the books that he read "had nothing to do with anything that mattered *now*." Although she considers him "homeless" and his soul a "vacuum," it is altogether to Walter's credit that he refuses membership in his mother's NOW generation.

Walter quietly but definitively rejects fellowship with mammon. When he tells his mother, "A woman of your generation . . . is better than a man of mine," it is not with the characteristic pride of O'Connor's young intellectuals, but an honest admission of limitation. He parodies the pronouncement of Jesus that the children of this genera-tion are wiser than the children of light and effectively judges both his mother and himself. To the whispered outrage of his mother's response, "I would be ashamed to say it!" he answers simply, "The only virtue of my generation . . . is that it ain't ashamed to tell the truth about itself." These words that terminate their interview are by no means self-righteous. The limitation that Walter admits is a mixture of freedom and determinism. He knows more certainly what he does *not* want to do than how to achieve what he wants. His confession nonetheless prepares his mother for the disquieting realization that comes to her through the martial words of a Father of the Church. She knows at the end of their conversation that her son has rejected wealth; what she has not learned is that he has secretly accepted Jesus as his Master.

Perhaps in the spirit of St. Jerome, whose letter to Heliodorus he has been reading, Walter amuses himself "writing letters to people he [does] not know and to the newspaper." That a twenty-eight-year-old man occupies himself with nothing but such trivia is no amusement to his mother. In fact, because he conceals his identity, it infuriates her all the more; his pastime is the kind of "peculiar, small, contemptible vice" that her father and grandfather would have avoided—apparently *in favor of* "great ones," rather than *as well as*. When Walter's mother reads Jerome's stern message to Heliodorus, who had abandoned his call to the hermitic life, she appreciates its fury but misses initially the ultimate source of its power. Jerome trumpets the summons to battle in the name of their General; and in language that has no doubt affected Walter, he calls Heliodorus an "effeminate soldier" for quitting the ramparts to hide in his father's house. "Arising finally from your nap, do you come to the battlefield!" Jerome inveighs. "Abandon the shade and seek the sun." What strikes Walter's mother at first as making "no sense for now" changes suddenly "with an unpleasant little jolt" into the disturbing insight that the General they were following into battle was Jesus! Walter knows himself well enough to admit that if he cannot yet "seek the sun," he can at least abandon the "shade" of avarice—which his mother still clings to. Her "unpleasant little" discovery, though, is too slight to jolt her from her furious allegiance to mammon. It is better to be a secret servant of the light than a forthright child of the shade. Knowing one's limitations is at least a remote preparation for the real battle.

3: The Collections

THE STRUCTURAL DYNAMISM OF THE WORD IS NOT UNI-
formly strong in O'Connor's earlier fiction; it nevertheless
appears as the unique aesthetic principle that her art was
building toward. Of the uncollected stories, "The Partridge
Festival" alone reveals the excellence of her typical
hermeneutic use of language; it was, however, written
during the consciously parabolic period of the second
collection. The revelatory power of the word is consistently the dramatic center of the stories of the two
collections. Whereas her characteristic technique is more
pronounced in *Everything That Rises Must Converge*, it is
perhaps more subtly effective in the earlier collection, *A
Good Man Is Hard to Find*.

I

It is a curious phenomenon that critics have generally
dealt successfully with the words and gestures of "A
Good Man Is Hard to Find," despite the subtlety of its
interpretive structure in comparison with the more blatant
use of word in "Revelation," which for obvious reasons I
consider to be O'Connor's prototypical hermeneutic
parable. Perhaps this can be attributed to the fact that
O'Connor herself provided an introduction to a reading of
the story which identifies the central word and gesture.[1]
Even though we have O'Connor's testimony that the
moment of grace in the story for her "is the Grandmother's recognition that the Misfit is one of her chil-

dren,"[2] criticism has not been victimized by the intentional fallacy: the power of the interpretive word itself is what makes the story so intelligible.

Though unambiguous in meaning, the title story of the first collection has been faulted on other grounds, most recently by Martha Stephens as typifying a conflict between comedy and seriousness that she feels afflicts even some of O'Connor's better stories. Stephens judges the climactic scene a failure due to "the fact that a tonal shift that occurs midway through the story finally runs out of control."[3] Aside from the conspicuous presence of what Stephens labels O'Connor's "formidable doctrine"—which, as we have noted, she ultimately rejects for philosophical reasons under the guise of literary terminology—she finds "the chief horror of the whole massacre scene" to be the way The Misfit's casual discussion of belief "is punctuated by his polite commands for the execution of the other members of the family."[4] Stephens's literary miscalculation results from her failure to observe the horror in the earlier scenes; her judgment that "there is everywhere in the first part of this story the most scrupulous comic realism"[5] simply will not stand under scrutiny. Although there is necessarily a shift in tone in the story, it is adequately foreshadowed in the sharply-limned irony of the introductory scenes; and it is the accident, not the appearance of The Misfit, that occasions the shift. (Recall the shocking understatement of the accident's effects, juxtaposing the "broken front brim" of the grandmother's hat with the children's mother, who "only had a cut down her face and a broken shoulder.") The story patently assumes that life suddenly explodes with the possibility of meaning, that the eschatological crisis does indeed intrude upon the commonplace; and as O'Connor so often observed, all one has to do is read the newspapers to verify this daily eruption of violence.

The principal irony of the earlier scenes is doubtlessly the revelation that the grandmother's unconscious desire to have her own way about the vacation (she wanted to go to East Tennessee rather than Florida) is responsible for the family tragedy: while they are still in Georgia, she directs them to a plantation that is actually in Tennessee. So shocked is she by the realization of her mistake that she upsets the cat's basket, creating the panic that causes the accident. There are many other narrative and descriptive elements, though, that anticipate the story's tragedy. The Misfit, known to be headed for Florida, is introduced in the first paragraph, in support of the grandmother's preference for a vacation in Tennessee. Her attire for the trip is so impeccably proper that "in case of an accident, anyone seeing her dead on the highway would know at once that she was a lady." Pointing out a small cemetery that they pass with "five or six graves" in it, the grandmother explains that it is an "old family burying ground . . . that belonged to the plantation." The grave-yard is of course just the size they will need at the end of the story if we take the "or six" as an ironic accommoda-tion of the baby. When they stop for lunch at The Tower, Red Sammy's wife interjects a harsh note of reality into a superficial exchange between her husband and the grand-mother when she warns, "It isn't a soul in this green world of God's that you can trust. . . . And I don't count nobody out of that, not nobody." It is "outside of Toomsboro" that the grandmother mistakenly recalls the plantation that they detour (permanently) to visit. And throughout the story until they are escorted off into the woods to be shot, John Wesley and June Star behave so hatefully that even The Misfit seems lovable by contrast.

For the first time in O'Connor's fiction, but hardly the last, a self-consciously demonic character opens up the possibilities of existence for the protagonist. Although it is the grandmother who urges The Misfit to pray and introduces Jesus into their conversation, The Misfit is the one who recalls how "Jesus thown everything off balance." He feels that like Jesus he has suffered undeservedly (hence his name), the only difference being that "He hadn't committed any crime" and they could prove at least one on The Misfit. What Jesus should not have done, The Misfit claims, was raise the dead: "If He did what He said, then it's nothing for you to do but thow away everything and follow Him, and if He didn't, then it's nothing for you to do but enjoy the few minutes you got left the best way you can—by killing somebody or burning down his house or doing some other meanness to him. No pleasure but meanness." Thus by his decision to kill the grandmother and her whole family The Misfit seems to deny that Jesus really had "raised the dead," while implying the opposite when he concludes later that "it's no real pleasure in life." The grandmother's response to the word that opens up a dimension of reality her vapid gentility is inclined to disregard is the perfect counterpart of The Misfit's. "Not knowing what she was saying," she mumbles a denial, "Maybe He didn't raise the dead," and then reaches out to The Misfit as if she actually believes "Jesus . . . raised the dead" when she acknowledges her responsibility for his sin, "Why you're one of my babies. You're one of my own children!" She is the mother of his sin inasmuch as she helped to make the world that created his need. To The Misfit her touch is like the bite of a snake. The gesture of recognition and acceptance provokes immediate violence.

The Misfit denies the resurrection in deed and thereby the possibility of ultimate meaning in life, yet seems in the end to imply a desire to accept it; he is at least painfully dissatisfied with the fruit of his choice. Although the grandmother seems initially to deny ultimate meaning in word, she plainly accepts it in both deed and word. The Misfit himself acknowledges how the extreme situation has revealed her essential goodness. "She would of been a good woman," he tells Bobby Lee, "if it had been somebody there to shoot her every minute of her life." Her appearance in death confirms the renewal implied in his words; her legs are crossed under her "like a child's" and "her face [is] smiling up at the cloudless sky." (Even Bailey had shown signs of filial piety under the threat of

death; the man who had just cursed his mother for
identifying The Misfit said affectionately as he left for the
woods, "I'll be back in a minute, Mamma, wait on me!")
Although it is The Misfit's word that illumines the
grandmother's option and ours—the promise of renewal
that belief in life offers—it is the grandmother's confession
that reveals a sure basis of human goodness, the admission
of our involvement in the sins of the world.

In "The River," the Reverend Bevel Summers, explain-
ing the effects of baptism to Harry Ashfield, assures him,
"You won't be the same again. . . . You'll count." Through
this simple but suggestive statement the story delineates
for the reader as well the ambience within which he
"counts," and it is obviously not merely baptism as
magical immersion or even fundamentalist sacrament that
makes the difference, as theological overinterpretation of
"The River" so often implies. The preacher is far from
simplistic in his explanation of the rite or of the
significance of the river itself. He begins with a clear
rejection of the self-centered concern with healing that has
obviously led to Mr. Paradise's cynicism. "If you ain't
come for Jesus, you ain't come for me," he insists. "If you
just come to see can you leave your pain in the river, you
ain't come for Jesus. You can't leave your pain in the
river. . . . I never told nobody that."
   The river and its rite are unequivocally symbolic.
"Listen to what I got to say, you people," the preacher
shouts, "There ain't but one river and that's the River of
Life, made out of Jesus' Blood. That's the river you have
to lay your pain in, in the River of Faith, in the River of
Life, in the River of Love, in the rich red river of Jesus'
Blood, you people!" The river of life that one enters
through baptism is the way of love and faith and pain that
leads to the Kingdom of Christ. And the reason why the
baptized Harry counts is precisely because the atmosphere
of belief provided by Mrs. Connin and the Reverend Bevel
Summers offers a total vision of life; Harry is introduced

to meaning that his parents' hedonism and sophistication are incapable of providing. One counts, the story announces, where concern is ultimate.

The two souvenirs that Harry preserves from the day in the country are emblematic of the integral concern that Mrs. Connin has shown him—"a red and blue flowered handkerchief" for his body and "The Life of Jesus Christ for Readers Under Twelve" for his spirit. The description of Mrs. Connin and the procession of her family with Harry to the river attest to the child's rite of passage from abandonment to total care. Mrs. Connin looms before Harry like "a speckled skeleton"; when she falls asleep on the bus, she whistles and blows "like a musical skeleton." And the procession made by the children and Mrs. Connin looks "like the skeleton of an old boat with two pointed ends, sailing slowly on the edge of the highway." The allusions to death and possibly also to the ark foreshadow the ending of the story, but more importantly they emphasize the process of Harry's passage through death to life that is at the heart of the story. He must leave the meaninglessness of his parents' apartment in order to count, and death in the guise of Mrs. Connin is the agent of his passage. She is of course the one who mentions and naively accepts the name that Harry takes as his title of passage—Bevel. For he has heard her refer to the Reverend Bevel Summers as a healer; and thus impishly, but with a wisdom beyond his years, he takes the name of the man who will heal him of his hunger for concern and who could possibly make even his mother well.

The desire to "count" permanently—as Harry never has in the "ashfield" of his parents' urban apartment—ultimately shapes his decision to return to the country and its river of life. The tonal contrast that names country over city as the place where Harry "counts" is drawn principally in terms of color and related contrasts. The difference is by no means a facile distinction between good and evil; rather, in the country there is the clarity of recognizable contrast. In the apartment everything is dark and gray, even the sun appears pale, "stained gray by the glass." The apartment is dark during the day because its adult inhabitants are night people; the family name indicates its characteristic desolation. Moreover, everything there is a joke: his mother's "illness" is a hangover; even Jesus Christ, Harry would have thought formerly, "was a word like 'oh' or 'damn' or 'God,' or maybe somebody who had cheated them out of something sometime." The country, on the other hand, is all oranges, greens, and yellows; the sun is a "white Sunday sun." Even though Mr. Paradise and the shoats roam the countryside, they stand in clear contrast to the preacher, Mrs. Connin, and the natural setting. Color sharpens meaning rather than blurs it.

Miles Orvell claims that "the story fails to convince us that the little boy has done anything but unfortunately confuse a literal meaning and a symbolic meaning; the atmosphere of the story is not 'liberated' sufficiently to accommodate the allegory."[6] Whatever the meaning of his second clause may be, the first misses altogether the story's brilliant application of generally accepted learning theory and reflects inadequate appreciation of the tonal differentiation between city and country. What is unmistakably important in any interpretive process is how the "world of the work" is understood by the protagonist, because it is through the eyes of the protagonist that *we* see his world if the tale enjoys basic artistic success. Harry's grasp of the preacher's language, happily for him, equates image and reality because this is the mode of preliterate apprehension. Suicide is obviously beyond Harry's intention; being in the water—more precisely, being received by the water—is what makes him count. (At home, when his mother had pulled him to a sitting position to question him about the preacher, the emptiness of her gesture and presumably of life with his parents is expressed in the reversal of the image: "he felt as it he had been drawn up from under the river.") The paradox of the story is that Harry's experience of the river yields a birth of reason inasmuch as "the river wouldn't have him." Its persistent rejection forces him to stop and think that "it's another joke, it's just another joke." Then he sees Mr. Paradise. Harry knows enough about hogs from his frightening experience at Mrs. Connin's to appreciate Jesus' having to drive the "crowd of pigs out of a man," and Mr. Paradise with the "purple bulge on his left temple" favors the shoat with an ear bitten off that has already scared Harry half to death. It is thus his fear of the evil Mr. Paradise, "like a giant pig bounding after him," and his effort to escape him that lead ironically to a happy death. Complete acceptance by the river is of course Harry's ultimate concern.

Although the description of Tom T. Shiftlet in "The Life You Save May Be Your Own" alludes superficially to Jesus—he comes a homeless man into the lives of needy people and performs a servant's role[7]—the total context of the story seems rather to demand the more obvious judgment that he is a confidence man. Even the most specific allusion to salvation, when Mr. Shiftlet raises his arms to embrace the expanse of the sunset and "his figure [forms] a crooked cross," leaves us with two serious doubts about his authenticity; it is after all a "crooked" cross and his arrival at "sunset" is more appropriate to the ambiguity surrounding the loosing of Satan, whose secular counterpart the con man is. Indeed the explicit bases for the struggle between Mr. Shiftlet and Lucynell Crater make it sufficiently clear that each is trying to con the other to satisfy a secret ambition: "She was ravenous for a son-in-law," and "he had always wanted an automobile but he had never been able to afford one before." Mr. Shiftlet's full intentions, however, are more artfully concealed. His goal is acknowledged only when he is driving away with daughter Lucynell, whereas the mother's need is stated bluntly even before her campaign is inaugurated. Imagery affords one earlier indication that successful repair of the car may be a major obstacle removed toward the realization of Mr. Shiftlet's real goal, as well as occasion for consummate self-satisfaction; when the automobile emerges noisily from the shed, to the accompaniment of daughter Lucynell's alleluia chorus of "Burrddttt! bddurrddtttt!" (her first word is absurd slang commentary on the con man's seriousness of purpose and ability to make the dumb talk), Mr. Shiftlet sits erect and triumphant in the driver's seat: "He had an expression of serious modesty on his face as if he had just raised the dead."

The quality of his personal revelation and philosophical reflection is confirmation enough of the confidence hypothesis. His penchant for moral platitudes undercuts even his modest attempts at personal honesty. Because Mr. Shiftlet has "only half an arm" in his left sleeve, the most salient feature of his initial description, we anticipate the disclosure that he is only half a man in spirit as well as in flesh. His own admission "I'm a man, . . . even if I ain't a whole one" refers only to his handicapped condition inasmuch as he concludes by asserting, "I got . . . a moral intelligence." His stare, however, indicates that even he is astonished by the utterance of this latter "impossible truth," and the assumption is not that "a moral intelligence" is foreign to man, only to Mr. Shiftlet. "Nothing is like it used to be, lady," he reminds Lucynell Crater, "the world is almost rotten." As for the doctor in Atlanta who had cut "the human heart . . . out of a man's chest and held it in his hand," Mr. Shiftlet hastens to assure her, "He don't know no more about it than you or me." Whereas the doctor's claim to know the heart as organ is analogous to Mr. Shiftlet's expertise as carpenter and mechanic, the ironic implication of Mr. Shiftlet's complaint is that he and Mrs. Crater may actually know more about the heart as restless spirit or demonic agent.

Mr. Shiftlet's closest approach to complete honesty disintegrates into rhetorical wonder. When he asks Mrs. Crater how she knows he has not lied about his identity, he confesses, "People don't care how they lie. Maybe the best I can tell you is, I'm a man." Yet he continues, "But listen lady, . . . what is a man?" Later, in apparent justification of his restlessness, he offers an hypothesis: "A man is divided into two parts, body and spirit. . . . The body, lady, is like a house: it don't go anywhere; but the spirit, lady, is like a automobile: always on the move, always. . . ." ⌊His linking man's spirit with mechanical transportation is clue enough to warn us that we cannot assume the human spirit always moves in the right direction.⌋ Indeed, Mr. Shiftlet's final destination —Mobile—seems intended as a pun on his lingering preference for perpetual motion, while the full humor of his reference to having "fought and bled in the Arm [sic] Service" lies in its tribute to his previous dedication to half-manhood.

Twice the directness of Lucynell Crater's language disturbs Mr. Shiftlet to the core—an acknowledgement both of the power of the word and of his reluctance to respond. Trying to persuade Mr. Shiftlet to remain with them, Lucynell Crater observes, "Lemme tell you something: there ain't any place in the world for a poor disabled friendless drifting man." "The ugly words," we are told, "settled in Mr. Shiftlet's head like a group of buzzards in the top of a tree." When the woman insists that seventeen-fifty is as high as she will go in sponsoring her daughter's weekend honeymoon, she adds, "That's all I got so it isn't any use you trying to milk me." Again, her choice of words seems to touch a sensitive chord: "Mr. Shiftlet was deeply hurt by the word 'milk.' " Although apparently closer to self-knowledge at the conclusion of the story, Mr. Shiftlet still prefers to flee the sting of the interpretive word.

Whereas the traffic safety slogan that Mr. Shiftlet passes on the highway—"Drive carefully. The life you save may be your own"—provides a title for the story and ironic commentary on his continued rejection of saving possibility, the dramatic center of the story, weak as it may seem, lies in the climactic exchange between the

confidence man and his youthful avatar. Giving a typically
insincere instruction in filial piety to the young runaway
he picks up on the road to Mobile, Mr. Shiftlet foolishly
applies to his abandoned mother the same epithet used of
his wife Lucynell just before he deserted her at The Hot
Spot—"angel of Gawd"—and the pharisaical expression
provokes a harsh judgment. The boy cries angrily, "You go
to the devil! . . . My old woman is a flea bag and yours is a
stinking pole cat!" There is an innate pull in man to deny
the most fundamental bonds of love. Hearing the ugly
truth of man's infidelity spoken baldly for once seems to
shock Mr. Shiftlet into an awareness of the hypocrisy that
had laced his sermon as it had his life. Yet the reader, like
Gertrude reacting to the player queen in *Hamlet*, knows
what the boy senses instinctively: the gentleman protests
too much. That the shock does not result in a genuine
change of heart is clear from the sequel. For the
turnip-shaped cloud, the guffawing peal of thunder and
fantastic raindrops become a "galloping shower" that
pursues Mr. Shiftlet into Mobile. Even if his prayer for the
purification of the earth does include himself in the
"slime" that needs to be washed away, Mr. Shiftlet is
obviously not ready to be cleansed.[8]

Besides the more conventional role of language in
interpretive dialogue, there are three occasions in this first
collection where words also take physical shape and
function as separate dramatic entities; they are forces to be
struggled with at least in the mind of the protagonist,
reminiscent of Rayber's experience in "The Barber." The
first of these reifications of language occurs in "A Stroke
of Good Fortune" where Ruby Hill, beset with obvious
signs of pregnancy and repeated words of revelation, seems
to grasp at almost any other explanation of her illness until
the echoes of truth pierce at last the protective layers of
her mind.

At the age of thirty-four, Ruby is already a short, fat
woman, "shaped nearly like a funeral urn." The image

anticipates the disclosure that Bill Hill, her husband, has
with her approval been "preventing" her body from
nurturing life—but not evidently with complete success.
She remembers with regret how her mother at the same
age had "looked like a puckered-up old yellow apple, sour,"
because of the eight children she had been forced to have:
"Her mother had got deader with every one of them."
Whereas pregnancy promises a renewal of human life,
Ruby instinctively wants to remain the vegetable that she
resembles in the story's first instructive simile. With a
collard leaf touching her cheek as she rests her bag of
groceries on the foyer table of the apartment building, her
head seems balanced "like a big florid vegetable at the top
of the sack." The association is less than pleasant to her
because Ruby feels that it is demeaning to serve collards
for her brother; after two years in the army he ought to
have outgrown his disgusting rural tastes. As she swipes the
leaf away, she mutters, " 'Collard greens,' . . . spitting the
word from her mouth . . . as if it were a poisonous seed."

Struggling up the stairs to her apartment, winded and
nauseated, she tries half-heartedly to uncover the mystery
of the pain in her stomach. The palmist, Madam Zoleeda,
had said she would have "a long illness," yet it would bring
her "a stroke of good fortune." So limited is Ruby's selfish
perspective that she hopes the "good fortune" will mean
"moving" to the suburbs where there are no stairs to
climb. The recurring pain frightens her though: "She had
thought the word *cancer* once and dropped it instantly
because no horror like that was coming to her because it
couldn't. The word came back to her immediately with the
pain but she slashed it in two with Madam Zoleeda. It will
end in good fortune. She slashed it twice through and then
again until there were only pieces of it that couldn't be
recognized."

As Ruby slowly, exhaustedly climbs the stairs, the
story's hermeneutic evidence mounts in inverse proportion
to her deceleration. Already breathless on the first flight,
Ruby decides she must rest. She sits on Hartley Gilfeet's

pistol! Even though his mother calls him "Little Mister Good Fortune," Ruby fails to draw any conclusions concerning her expected "good fortune." Mr. Jerger, the elderly second-floor resident who always has a question for everyone, asks Ruby if she knows "what great birthday" it is. Anyone married to a man from Florida, he says, ought to know that it is the day Ponce de León landed there, "looking for the fountain of youth." Interested obviously in whether he had found it, but ignorant of history, Ruby is led reluctantly to Mr. Jerger's lesson for the day—the solution to her anxiety about the burden of motherhood. Although Ponce de León had not found the mystical fountain, Mr. Jerger claims to have "drunk of it." The only youth worth maintaining, a youthful heart, is of no interest to Ruby. Her good friend Laverne Watts on the third floor delivers a far less subtle message. "Swaying with her stomach stuck out," she sings gleefully about Ruby's symptoms, "Put them all together, they spell MOTHER! MOTHER!"

It is ultimately the conjunction of words spoken by Laverne Watts and Madam Zoleeda that provides sluggish Ruby with the definitive diagnosis of her condition. Hartley Gilfeet (the fetal implication of his surname has been noted), rounding the bend in the stairs, collides with Ruby: "A charging chipmunk face crashed into her and rocketed through her head, smaller and smaller into a whirl of dark." As she is stunned into insensibility, her fifth-floor neighbor's "Little Mister Good Fortune" seems to fade with her into the darkness of embryonic expectation. When Ruby regains awareness, gazing back into the "dark hold" of the stairwell where her journey of discovery had begun, her words of recognition echo revelation received if not accepted through the cavernous stairwell, "Good Fortune, . . . Baby."

Since Ruby keeps referring to her brother Rufus as "an enfant"—"she saw him waiting out nowhere before he was born, just waiting, waiting to make his mother, only thirty-four, into an old woman"—the story's aesthetic logic seems reduced to this humorous syllogism: Rufus is coming, but Rufus is a baby, therefore a baby is coming. As the echoes in the stairwell jeer "Good Fortune, Baby" back at her, Ruby identifies the feeling in her stomach "as if it were out nowhere in nothing, out nowhere, resting and waiting, with plenty of time." If the convergence of evidence is taken seriously, her "enfant" will probably be twins. The climb to recognition had begun with a pistol under Ruby (as blatant a phallic reference perhaps as the name of the bible salesman in "Good Country People") and ends with Hartley himself, galloping up the stairs "with *two* pistols leveled" (my emphasis). Laverne Watts had said, "I bet it's not one, I bet it's two"; but more tellingly still, Ruby experiences a pain "like a piece of something pushing something else." That Ruby's pregnancy will yield *for her* something less than "a stroke of good fortune" lies in the ironic repetition of her image of her mother's last pregnancy; what rests "out nowhere in nothing" is waiting only to make Ruby into an older woman. Inasmuch as Ruby already has less life in herself through self-indulgence before the advent of her first child than her mother did after eight, the story strongly suggests that one gets "deader" by preventing life than by giving it.

When critics, with varying degrees of insistence, decide that they discern an author's self-portrait in his works, the designation is usually less than flattering. Stanley Edgar Hyman considers Hulga in "Good Country People" O'Connor's "cruelist self-caricature"[9] and the child in "A Temple of the Holy Ghost" as "a portrait of the artist as a sardonic twelve-year-old girl."[10] Martha Stephens, after noting the Catholic references in the latter story, rephrases Hyman's statement as a query: "Who, given such details as these, can keep from seeing this story as a portrait of the artist as a young girl?"[11] But even Stephens's question seems tainted with autobiographical implications that are more distracting than helpful. O'Connor's judicious protestation that the artist needs to write about what he knows—"he cannot choose what he is able to make live"[12] —would suggest that all her fiction, like any other writer's, is to the extent it lives the portrait of an artist; and her honesty about human limitation implies a self-knowledge that could wisely illumine any countryside. Narrower autobiographical insinuations depreciate the universality of her art. Moreover, "A Temple of the Holy Ghost" is one of O'Connor's most positive and reassuring pictures of human potentiality; the full implications of the story could readily lead to justifiable accusations of uncharacteristic self-praise.

In this delightful tale of preadolescent madness, a circus hermaphrodite utters the word that transforms a hateful child into a maturing adolescent who is well on the road toward accepting herself and her world for what they are and what they can be. Physical deformity is the story's image for spiritual limitation; admitting and accepting that deformity is the avenue to possibility. The freak's confession and warning relayed to the child by Susan and Joanne—"God made me thisaway and if you laugh He may strike you the same way"—returns to her dreamy imagination as a litany of self-acceptance and a hymn of gratitude; it becomes eventually the basis for her act of hope in the future.

Descriptive emphasis in the story is on physical abnormality. Unlike the older girls whose developing sexuality confines their attention narcissistically to themselves (they put on lipstick and high heels and pass slowly in front of the hall mirror "to get a look at their legs"), the child's attention is directed indiscriminately toward the humorous disproportions of others. Although she convulses with laughter at the way Mr. Cheatam, Alonzo Myers, and the two Wilkinses look, her sassiest comments pretend to cut through appearances to inner reality. She considers the older girls to be "practically morons" after observing their behavior, and when Wendell supposes that the *Tantum ergo* "must be Jew singing," she calls him a "big dumb Church of God ox" and insists that the boys are "stupid idiots;" she confounds the cook by asserting rashly that God could strike her deaf, dumb, and blind and she "would still be smarter than some." When finally she comes to pray for an altered disposition, it is for the deformity of her own heart that she is more concerned—another assurance that physical abnormality is the story's metaphor for willful deviation of the spirit.

The child's prayerful ruminations prior to learning about the hermaphrodite offer an instructive contrast to the modesty of final possibility. When she imagines that what happens inside the adult tents at the circus "concerned medicine," she thinks of being a doctor; then for no apparent reason her ambition shifts to engineering. But watching the arc of the revolving searchlight, she feels that she would have to be "much more than just a doctor or an engineer"—perhaps a saint, except that she was consumed by the sin of pride, or at least a martyr, "if they killed her quick." She rehearses her martyrdom in glamorous De Mille fashion, but each time she reaches the entrance to paradise, she returns to the lions that had cowered submissively in her presence, a foreshadowing of her final realization that there is no road forward for her unless she subdues the lions of pride in herself—lies, sloth, sass, and deliberate ugliness.

Contemplating the Benediction host in the convent chapel, she recalls again the words of the hermaphrodite—"I don't dispute it; this is the way He wanted me to be"—and the association of host and hermaphrodite is a reminder that God himself, becoming man, accepted the limitations of the human condition and in becoming bread for remembrance submitted to the lowly dimensions of everyday food. The vision that faith supplies to the child's faltering senses—in the words of the *Tantum Ergo*, "*Preastet fides supplementum/ Sensuum defectui*"—converts Joanne's and Susan's joke about being Temple One and Temple Two into an act of genuine self-acceptance and hope for the future. She has risen through physical limitation to an acknowledgement of spiritual fault, reassured by the realization that the spirit can indeed transcend the limits of the flesh. Her final prayer is pure, though modest, hope. "Hep me," she prays, "not to be so mean. . . . Hep me not to give her so much sass. Hep me not to talk like I do." "A Temple of the Holy Ghost" is much more than a story in which deformity demonstrates simply "that man's condition is normally corrupt and that he is better off in accepting it,"[13] as Carter Martin states. In the likeness of the hermaphrodite, the child comes—as each of us must—to realize what her limitations are but, more importantly, what she can accomplish despite them.

"The Artificial Nigger" is an extraordinarily nuanced parable, built on a Dantean frame of images,[14] which dramatizes a theme analogous to the Greek tragic motif that wisdom comes through suffering. The action of mercy, O'Connor proposes, grows out of agony. The experience of mercy is indeed nobler than the advent of that wisdom which the Greeks conceived as passage from ignorance to knowledge. Mercy is in the order of salvation, of radical human transformation, and there is redemption for man only if his stance in relation to the mystery of existence is one of integral humility.

Although "The Artificial Nigger" is generally considered one of O'Connor's best stories, it has been one of her most seriously misinterpreted, and even its advocates feel obliged to justify the blunt theological language of its resolution.[15] Orvell's suggested explanation of the penultimate paragraph, however, that "the experience of grace is so uncommon as to warrant some emphasis"[16] is the kind of "possible" justification that obfuscates rather than clarifies. The "experience" of grace in O'Connor's works is certainly not uncommon; neither is its "acceptance" for that matter, though it is rarer. Orvell is perhaps closer to the truth when he suggests that, because the story is "freighted with sociological and political overtones," O'Connor may have felt that the theological implications would be overlooked. There is indeed manuscript evidence that she expanded the first two paragraphs to four besides significantly amplifing the description of the religious experience at its conclusion.[17]

Explicit theological language is commonplace in O'Connor's fiction—the Bible Belt is after all her "countryside"—but it is unusual for the images to seem so obtrusive. If one insists that the quality of Mr. Head's reflection on his experience is beyond the depth of his personality, it is equally true that O'Connor does not attempt here to preserve a narrative tone consistent with either character's mentality. Whatever her reason, she maintains an omniscient viewpoint that exhibits a strong authorial presence from the very beginning. A narrative that can sustain the explicit typology of "the great guides of men," moreover, can justifiably situate Mr. Head's sin in the history of the race. Conscious of the story's mythic dimensions, the author explains Mr. Head's "look of composure and of ancient wisdom": "He might have been Vergil summoned in the middle of the night to go to Dante, or better, Raphael, awakened by a blast of God's light to fly to the side of Tobias." So at the end of the story she tells us what "he understood" and "he realized"; most importantly, the language of "mercy," "agony," and "the sin of Adam" is in perfect harmony with the universal religious implications of the story's central symbol.

Building to the interpretive language of its recognition scene, the story enjoys the classical unity of beginning, middle, and end. The preparation establishes the problem, the journey unfolds its dimensions, the return—both recognition and homecoming—proclaims its resolution. Mr. Head conceives the trip with Nelson to Atlanta "in moral terms," as "a lesson that the boy would never forget." Since Nelson says that this is his second trip to the city (Atlanta was his birthplace), Mr. Head intends for him "to find out from it that he had no cause for pride merely because he had been born in a city." A specific lesson that he wants Nelson to learn is that "the city is not a great place"; in the language of prejudice, the only one that Mr.

Head knows, the boy must see that the city is a "nigger heaven" and afterwards "be content to stay at home for the rest of his life." The actual object of Mr. Head's "moral lesson" is to convince his grandson of the superiority of his knowledge. "Only with years," Mr. Head feels, "does a man enter into that calm understanding of life that makes him a suitable guide for the young." But Nelson, "a child who was never satisfied until he had given an impudent answer," can hardly imagine his grandfather's "third trip" to the city as a sufficiently impressive record to qualify him for the role of sage cicerone. "I will've already been there twict and I ain't but ten," he boasts. The pride of age is pitted against the perversity of youth.

The journey through the city is an interesting counterpoint of lost way and found dependence. Convinced that Nelson does not even know what a Negro is (there has not been one in their county for twelve years), Mr. Head asks the boy to identify "a huge coffee-colored man" passing in the aisle. He makes successive guesses of "a man," "a fat man," and "an old man" before his grandfather announces triumphantly, "That was a nigger"—a brilliant illustration of the psychological truth that one has to be educated to prejudice. Because Nelson is embarrassed by his "ignorance" and feels that the Negro "deliberately walked down the aisle to make a fool of him," he understands why his grandfather dislikes them. Later, when Nelson lunges forward at the conductor's announcement of the Emory University stop—"Firstoppppppmry"—his grandfather, remembering a previous mistake, orders him to "keep [his] seat. . . . For the first time in his life, he understood that his grandfather was indispensable to him." Ashamed at his emotional attraction to a black woman who tells them to follow the tracks back to the city, Nelson takes hold of his grandfather's hand, "a sign of dependence that he seldom showed."

Reversing this pattern of deepening dependence is the accumulation of evidence damaging to Mr. Head's leadership. Under his supposed guidance they leave their lunch on the train and even lose their way in the city a second time by following the trolley tracks in the wrong direction. Wanting "to teach a child a lesson he won't forget, particularly when the child is always reasserting his position with some new impudence," Mr. Head momentarily abandons the sleeping boy to observe his frightened reaction, but effectively loses his grandson for what seems an eternity. The panic-stricken Nelson collides with an elderly woman, and Mr. Head foolishly denies any relationship with the boy for fear that he will have to pay for the woman's injuries. The crowd is "so repulsed by a man who would deny his own image and likeness" that they desert him.

Estranged totally by denial and refusal to forgive, Mr. Head and Nelson wander lost until the old man, terrified at the thought of remaining in the city overnight, has the humility to admit, "I'm lost!" As they follow directions to a suburban station, they experience the action of mercy that is both recognition of sin and humble homecoming. Confronted by "the artificial nigger," the story's potent symbol, Nelson and Mr. Head exchange mutual words of self-revelation and forgiveness. Their own torment is projected perfectly into the "wild look of misery" that "the chipped eye" and "angle he was cocked at" gave the lawn statuette. Mr. Head equivalently confesses awareness of his personal sin of disdain by rejecting the agonizing excess of discrimination. There is as little need to call a man "a nigger," he realizes, as there is to add artificial misery to all that exists already. "They ain't got enough real ones here," he says, "they got to have an artificial one." This excess is a denial of reality just as his excessive desire to prove his superiority to Nelson was a denial of his common bond with ignorant humanity. Nelson responds with a corresponding acceptance of his genuine limitations: "Let's go home before we get ourselves lost again." Once home, and grateful for the experience of mercy, he renounces his perverse title to the "other" visit to the city. "I'm glad I've went once," he mutters, "but I'll never go

back again!" They had both claimed to possess knowledge
of the city which they did not have; they leave it with an
awareness of mercy even though they had been lost in sin.
The action of mercy that the story dramatizes so effectively is the experience of forgiveness; the agony that is the
root of forgiveness is the prior acknowledgment of shared
fault.

"A Circle in the Fire" investigates the nature of man's
stewardship of the earth in the purifying fire of eschata-
logical crisis. Although Powell Boyd is the principal
antagonist of the story, the pervasive hermeneutic struggle
results from the opposing world views of Mrs. Cope and
the wife of her hired man, Mrs. Pritchard. Mrs. Cope insists
that she "can always find something to be thankful for":
in fact, she says a prayer of thanksgiving every day. "Think
of all we have. Lord," she tells Mrs. Pritchard, "we have
everything." Her eucharistic refrain, however, seems
designed mainly to counteract the "calamitous stories"
that Mrs. Pritchard thrives on. Gratitude for little things
aside, she prefers to cope with genuine misfortune by
keeping it at the safe distance of "poor Europeans" in
Siberian boxcars. Later, responding to Powell Boyd's
announcement of his father's death, she sounds "as if
death were always an unusual thing" when she says,
"Dead. Well I declare." Mrs. Pritchard, on the other hand,
"would go thirty miles for the satisfaction of seeing
anybody laid away." Her current preoccupation is with the
bizarre account of how a "seventh or eighth cousin by
marriage" not only gave birth to a child while in an iron
lung but also presumably had conceived in it. "Look like
to me if I was in one of them, I would leave off . . . how
you reckon they . . .?" Mrs. Pritchard conjectures as Mrs.
Cope rhapsodizes about gratitude.
    The truth of the matter is that Mrs. Cope is thankful
because until the present *she* has been in control of her
own limited world: "I have the best kept place in the
county and do you know why? Because I work," she

reminds Mrs. Pritchard. And although she claims, "I'm not always looking for trouble, I take it as it comes," she has suffered no misfortune worse than nut grass and lazy help. "Her negroes were as destructive and impersonal as the nut grass." Mrs. Pritchard's early warning about misfortune "If it all come at oncet sometime," interrupted by Mrs. Cope's foolish "It doesn't all come at once," is not completed until after Powell Boyd and his companions have already begun their systematic harassment of the farm. "There ain't a thing you can do about it," she then informs Mrs. Cope, and her full statement represents the story's definitive word about the finality of the eschatological crisis.

When Powell Boyd returns to the farm with his friends from the Atlanta housing development, it is because he remembers the place as having everything that his deprived circumstances in the city did not provide. For Powell, the freedom of its pasture and woods possesses the aura of heaven: "He said when he died he wanted to come here!" W. T. Harper tells Mrs. Cope. Powell has come to take possession of his kingdom; this is made perfectly clear by the repeated imagery of enclosure that builds eventually into the image of the title, a circle in the fire, when frustrated desire becomes destruction. "One of Powell's eyes [seems] to be making a circle of the place," while the other focuses on Mrs. Cope. Powell's stare seems "to pinch her like a pair of tongs." As he sits on a lawn chair, awaiting Mrs. Cope's stingy offering of Coca Cola and crackers, Powell looks "as if he [is] trying to enclose the whole place in one encircling stare."

Despite Mrs. Cope's protestations, the vexing evidence of misfortune coming all "at oncet" begins to mount. Since the boys smoke and her principal worry is "about fires in her woods," she insists that they camp in the field next to the house rather than in the barn or the woods; they cannot ride the horses because they might get hurt. When Mrs. Cope receives the report that they have ridden bareback all afternoon and entered the barn at night, she responds vehemently, " 'I cannot have this,' and her expression [is] the same as when she tore at the nut grass." The climactic moment of provocation is an unconscionable act of vandalism; the boys burn Mrs. Cope's woods so that they will not be there to miss. "If this place was not here any more," Powell tells Garfield and W. T., "you would never have to think of it again."

Mrs. Cope must not only accept the truth of Mrs. Pritchard's warning but also the loss of her prize possession. Even W. T. Harper, described with evangelical propriety as "that there little one," seemed to understand stewardship far better than Mrs. Cope when he uttered the judgment repeated to her by Mrs. Pritchard, "Man, Gawd owns them woods and her too." Incessantly prattling about her sense of gratitude, Mrs. Cope nonetheless managed to live as if not even God, who had given, had the right to take away. Mrs. Pritchard's recurring physical "misery in [the] face" (Her abscessed teeth) becomes Mrs. Cope's permanent expression of spiritual misery, her fellowship with disinherited man. She could not have known what thanksgiving actually entailed because she had never shared the common plight of man. The experience of misery is a prelude to genuine humanity because misery is the effect of sin and no one can escape its consequences.[18] Although the child Sally Virginia's misery is "new" because she has lost only a playground, her dispossessed mother's is "old": "It looked as if it might have belonged to anybody, a Negro or a European or to Powell himself." The quintessential human experience is dispossession rather than possession.

The story's final simile from the Book of Daniel is by no means the gratuitous addition that some critics have claimed. The striking parallels between the story and chapter 3 of Daniel clarify the manner in which we are to interpret the end of the narrative. Nebuchadnezzar, king of Babylon, constructs an idol of gold and orders the people to worship it; Mrs. Cope has made a golden idol of her woods and, although adoration is beyond her aim, she has equivalently asked the three youths to acknowledge its sacredness by leaving it undefiled. In the biblical narrative, the three Jewish men, Shadrach, Meshach, and Abed-nego refuse to comply with the king's order, are thrown into the fiery furnace, but are protected from the flames by an angel of God; impressed by the power of their God, Nebuchadnezzar turns from idolatry to worship the Lord. O'Connor's ironic variation is that her youths themselves destroy the idol of human possessions, but are preserved from new misery "in the circle" of deprivation they have always known. Like their Jewish counterparts, they not only refuse to adore the idol of man but also occasion the idolater's revelation. Unlike their biblical types—and this is the full irony of their "few wild high shrieks of joy"—the boys are more demonic than angelic because of their deliberate act of violence. If the conclusion of O'Connor's story refrains from explicit statement of Mrs. Cope's acceptance of that revelation, there is little doubt from the expression on her face that she has received the message.[19] The subtle significance of the biblical parallel is that it suggests rather than asserts the expectation of conversion.

Language in Flannery O'Connor's parables does not always achieve its effect on protagonist and reader in the same way. In "A Late Encounter with the Enemy," the word that specifically illumines our existence executes generic judgment on George Poker Sash. In yet another of O'Connor's instructive uses of reified language, the graduation oratory that "General" Sash is subjected to becomes a dreary procession of the personified demons of his past.

George Poker Sash, despite his one hundred and four years, never doubts that he will live till his granddaughter's graduation. "Living had got to be such a habit with him that he couldn't conceive of any other condition." He would never have consented to attend though "if she had not promised to see to it that he sit on the stage. He liked to sit on any stage. He considered that he was still a very handsome man." He likes to be seen and to see—"the

pretty girls." Sally Poker Sash's reason for wanting him to
attend is less specific but equally demeaning. Graduating
from college at the age of sixty-two, after twenty summer
sessions spent fulfilling requirements that had not been law
when she began teaching, "she wanted to show what she
stood for, or, as she said, 'what all was behind her,' and
was not behind them. This *them* was not anybody in
particular. It was just all the upstarts who had turned the
world on its head and unsettled the ways of decent living."
She planned to stand on the platform graduation day,
holding her head high as if to say, "See him! See him! My
kin, all you upstarts! Glorious upright old man standing
for the old traditions! Dignity! Honor! Courage! See him!"
Once she had dreamed ominously that she screamed, "See
him! See him!" and turned to discover the old man naked
in his wheel chair except for the general's hat. The night
before her graduation the same dream punctuates a fitful
sleep, but she awakens each time "just before she turned
her head to look at him behind her."

George Poker Sash had never been more than a major in
the Civil War. He is too old now to remember what his
rank was; he does not even remember the war. He has no
use for history "because he never [expects] to meet it
again." History for him is "a dreary black procession of
questions about the past"; he likes parades, not proces-
sions, because parades are associated with life. It was on
the occasion of the premiere of a great Civil War epic in
Atlanta (O'Connor undoubtedly has *Gone With the Wind*
in mind)—the "only event in the past that had any
significance for him"—that he had been dubbed a general
to add prestige to the celebration and had been given the
name Tennessee Flintrock Sash; even at ninety-two he was
spry enough to screech at the audience: "How I keep so
young, . . . I kiss all the pretty girls." Sally Poker knows
that the name and rank are fictitious, but by the time she
announces his attendance at the graduation to the Dean
she has glorified her own past enough to refer to her
grandfather as "General Tennessee Flintrock Sash of the

Confederacy." Both Sally and her grandfather have learned to feed their vanity by exploiting the past.

Although certain "words" from the graduation address cast specific light on the meaning of George Poker Sash's late encounter and thus on the meaning of the story, unquestionable emphasis within the story is given to their overall effect upon him. They are all apparently related to history. By the time the ceremonies begin, "General" Sash has already begun his encounter with death. Sally Poker has had to break from the procession to rescue her grandfather from the sun by a Coca-Cola machine where he had been left hatless by her irresponsible nephew John Wesley. The unnecessary exposure has a fatal effect on the old man: "[He] felt as if there were a little hole beginning to widen in the top of his head." It is through this widening hole that first the music and then even the procession itself seem to want to enter. As for the oration about history there is no seeming: "The General made up his mind he wouldn't listen, but the words kept seeping in through the little hole in his head." One apothegm partially invades his consciousness; it is a variation on Santayana's dictum about the necessity of repeating the forgotten past: "If we forget our past, . . . we won't remember our future and it will be as well for we won't have one."

George Poker Sash's primary hermeneutic experience, though, is of "the hole . . . letting the words he heard into the dark places of his brain. He heard the words, Chickamauga, Shiloh, Johnston, Lee, and he knew he was inspiring all these words that meant nothing to him. He wondered if he had been a general at Chickamauga or at Lee. . . . Old words began to stir in his head as if they were trying to wrench themselves out of place and come to life." The "long finger" of "slow black music" that makes its way into his head probes "various spots that were words, letting in a little light on the words and helping them to live." But when he says, "Dammit! I ain't going to have it!" whatever life the music was letting in to revitalize his memory is quenched, and the words become inexorable bullets of judgment from an invisible enemy—history—that should actually have been George Poker Sash's true friend. On a level close to literal, the words are the vanity of a fabricated past. More profoundly, they represent the past itself as opportunity regrettably lost.

Finally the words bring death to a man whose failure to understand the past has deprived him of any future. Just before he dies, the words, "coming at him like musket fire," riddle his body "in a hundred places with sharp stabs of pain." The places and faces he had used for vanity's sake rush at him "as if the past were the only future now and he had to endure it." "General" Sash has lived for so long off of history without having any genuine sense of its meaning that the words of revelation are never more than a final enemy he succumbs to; and Sally Poker Sash discovers too late that history has tricked her worse than her dreams, for the object of her false pride is not even a naked body—only a corpse.

The antagonist in "Good Country People" is introduced into the conflict by a mother who sees similarities between a stranger and her child. When the young Bible salesman, Manley Pointer, announces that he is dedicating his life to "Chrustian service" since what remains of it may be cut short because of a heart condition, Mrs. Hopewell likens him to Hulga, whose weak heart has kept her from a more active life at a university; and so Mrs. Hopewell invites him to dinner. Anyway she has a weakness for "good country people," who to her are "the salt of the earth."

Asked by Manley Pointer to go on a picnic, Hulga imagines herself seducing him because she is convinced that his country goodness is as artificial as her leg. When their actual conversation in the barn loft turns to God and salvation, Hulga, presuming that she will no doubt shock him, reminds him that she does not believe in God. In her gnostic economy of salvation, she obviously is saved and he is damned. But "salvation" is only a way of speaking for Hulga. "We are all damned," she insists, "but some of us have taken off our blindfolds and see that there's nothing to see. It's a kind of salvation." She is without illusions, or so she has deluded herself into thinking. "I'm one of those people who see *through* to nothing," she claims rashly. There is of course one very simple fact that Hulga should have seen if she had not already ruled out the possibility of seeing anything; the apparently innocent young man is, in fact, seducing her.

The heart-mind dichotomy is a crucial interpretive strand anticipating the story's final revelation. Hulga has spent her whole life developing her mind to the exclusion of her heart, so that her weak heart is clearly and ironically more than a physical disability. Although she considers Manley Pointer's kisses "an unexceptional experience," it is evident that her long inactive heart would like to function. Yet, the "extra surge of adrenalin" that they produce in her goes directly to the brain. When she responds to his kisses, her mind never once loses its ascendancy over her feelings. And when Manley Pointer acknowledges the "truth" about her artificial leg—it is what makes her different from everyone else—her heart seems to stop beating altogether, leaving "her mind to pump her blood." His suggestion that she prove her love for him by showing him where the artificial limb joins on shocks her not because of its obscenity (after all "it joins on . . . only at the knee"), but because "she [is] as sensitive about the artificial leg as a peacock about his tail." As he removes the leg and she experiences that unfamiliar sensation of dependence (as if she loses her life and finds it again completely in him), her brain seems to stop working too and "to be about some other function that it was not very good at." Since the mind, obviously, cannot replace the heart, Hulga is defenseless in a moment of extreme need; all of her vital functions appear to have ceased.

Totally helpless, she is the epiphany of pathetic humanity with divine aspirations. Fittingly, Manley Pointer becomes a *magus* presenting appropriate gifts—a flask of whiskey, playing cards with obscene pictures, and contraceptives. The heinousness of her pretensions is visible in the degradation of his offerings. Hulga, mesmerized and motionless, asks desperately, "Aren't you just good country people?" Her humiliation is not complete, or the revelation exhausted, until Manley Pointer spells out for her the extent of his deception. He has a collection of "interesting things" that he has stolen from his victims, and there is no hope of catching him because he uses a different name at each call and moves quickly from one place to another. In a final crushing blow to Hulga's pride, he reveals the depth of her judgment: "You ain't so smart. I been believing in nothing ever since I was born."

In the original typescript of *A Good Man Is Hard to Find* sent to Harcourt, Brace and World, "Good Country People" was placed at the end of the collection; perhaps in keeping with the cycle's quest for a "good man," O'Connor wanted to frame her collection by ending the volume with a title paralleling the lead story's use of "good." Its removal to the penultimate place, however, permits the collection to end on a more affirmative note inasmuch as the search for a good man bears late fruit in the appearance of "The Displaced Person," analogous to the eleventh-hour conversion of the grandmother in "A Good Man Is Hard to Find." In reversing the position of the last two stories, O'Connor added two concluding paragraphs to "Good Country People" which happily provide the reader with a frame of reference for grounding his estimate of the encounter between Hulga and the demonic Bible salesman. Mrs. Freeman, the nosey but nonetheless good country woman who works for Mrs. Hopewell, offers rustic wisdom mixed with honest self-knowledge. The opening paragraph of the story describes Mrs. Freeman as having three expressions: neutral, "that she wore when she was alone"; reverse, which "she seldom used . . . because it was not often necessary for her to retract a statement"; and forward, which "was steady and driving like the advance of a heavy truck." In the framing last paragraphs, she and Mrs. Hopewell are "digging up onions" as Manley Pointer emerges from the woods and heads across the meadow toward the highway. Mrs. Freeman's gaze drives "forward" to touch the fleeing suitor, and as she turns her attention back to her work, her judicious observation affirms the realism of her customary preoccupation with "infections," "deformities," and "assaults": "Some can't be that simple. . . . I know I never could." Good country people are not simple-minded innocents, as Mrs. Hopewell seemed to imply but, like Mrs. Freeman, people who know an "evil-smelling onion shoot" when they handle one.

Manley Pointer, fetishist masking as "salt of the earth," leaves with the artificial leg that was personal enough to have been Hulga's soul and the glasses that were her only claim to sight. Hulga's punishment for colossal pride is a literal realization of her wishes. She is as close to the Nothingness she sought to grasp as is retributively possible. Claiming to have seen through reality to nothing, she is stripped of her emblems of specious dignity by the one she had hoped to seduce. "Her icy blue eyes," seeing "green swelling lakes" instead of the "two pink-speckled hillsides" in front of the barn, seem frozen now "with the look of someone who has achieved blindness by an act of will and means to keep it." Hulga had imagined that the denial of reality was a prerogative of the enlightened mind, never suspecting that the demonic heart could reach the same conclusion. And for all her education she cannot tell a con man from good country people. Hulga's earlier indictment of her mother—"Do you ever look inside and see what you are *not*? God!"—returns to her own condemnation as the rural Prometheus steals the fire from her self-acclaimed Olympian mind.

Few stories of O'Connor's can boast such a superlative single reading as Sister M. Joselyn's analysis of the thematic centers in "The Displaced Person."[20] She shows

conclusively how the peacock and Mr. Guizac and their
analogue, Christ, draw corresponding reactions from the
principal characters on a descending scale from love to
hate. None of the major critics has done as much for this
concluding story of the first collection; Driskell and
Brittain even allow their principle of aesthetic harmony to
dictate an unacceptable interpretation of the spiritual fate
of Mrs. McIntyre and particularly of Mrs. Shortley.[21]

Words are once again reified, linking personal trauma
with history and myth. Mrs. Shortley, obsessed with fear
of her husband's dismissal in favor of the Guizacs and
possibly a second displaced Polish family, anticipates a
confrontation of languages that relates the Tower of Babel
to Auschwitz:

> She began to imagine a war of words, to see the Polish
> words and the English words coming at each other,
> stalking forward, not sentences, just words, gabble
> gabble gabble, flung out high and shrill and stalking
> forward and then grappling with each other. She saw the
> Polish words, dirty and all-knowing and unreformed,
> flinging mud on the clean English words until everything
> was equally dirty. She saw them all piled up in a room,
> all the dead dirty words, theirs and hers too, piled up
> like the naked bodies in the newsreel.

Although Mrs. Shortley "felt that religion was essentially for those people who didn't have the brains to avoid
evil without it," she tries to arouse fundamentalist fears of
"foreign" religion in order to protect herself and Mr.
Shortley from economic displacement by the more effi-
cient Mr. Guizac. "I would suspicion salvation got from
the devil," she responds ineffectually to Mrs. McIntyre,
whose exclamation "That man is my salvation!" has
already exposed her bourgeois preoccupation with material
things and concomitant immunity to religious provocation.
Pushed to an extreme of desperation, Mrs. Shortley pours
over the Apocalypse and quotes from the Prophets: "She
saw plainly that the meaning of the world was a mystery

that had been planned and she was not surprised to suspect that she had a special part in the plan because she was strong." Her business, in blunt terms, is "to watch the priest" who had arranged the placement of the Guizacs. "Here he was," she reflected, "leading foreigners over in hoards to places that were not theirs, to cause disputes, to uproot niggers, to plant the Whore of Babylon in the midst of the righteous!"

Urged by the voice accompanying her Sunday afternoon vision, she ironically predicts the manner of her own self-inflicted punishment and death. Alone in the pasture, she speaks apparently for her own benefit but is deaf to the warning. "The children of wicked nations will be butchered," she prophesies. "Legs where arms should be, foot to face, ear in the palm of hand. Who will remain whole? Who will remain whole? Who?" Because she had tried to displace the Guizacs, she is displaced, according to the acknowledged pattern of retribution in the story.[22] The displacers are the truly displaced persons. Refusing to accept her own displacement, she forces a hurried departure of her family before the dawn of the day Mr. Shortley will be given his month's notice. To the repetition of his poignant "Where we going?" she is butchered by the stroke her frenzied haste has caused: "She suddenly grabbed Mr. Shortley's elbow and Sarah Mae's foot at the same time and began to tug and pull on them as if she were trying to fit the two extra limbs onto herself. . . . She thrashed forward and backward, clutching at everything she could get her hands on and hugging it to herself, Mr. Shortley's head, Sarah Mae's leg, the cat, a wad of white bedding, her own big moon-like knee."

Even as her fierce expression fades "into a look of astonishment" and she dies, her daughters think that she is joking. "They didn't know," we are told a bit pointedly, "that she had had a great experience or ever been displaced in the world from all that belonged to her." The final sentence of this first section, reporting that in death Mrs. Shortley "seemed to contemplate for the first time the tremendous frontiers of her true country," can hardly indicate conversion or spiritual renewal. Rather, in view of the violent effect of her stroke, it discloses the consternation of one who is stunned by the realization that her actual part in the planned mystery of the world was totally different from her own self-righteous projection of it. Death is the "true country" that reveals the mystery formerly hidden from her. If the language appears disproportionately forceful in relation to Mrs. McIntyre's apocalypse, we must keep in mind that this was the conclusion of the story O'Connor originally published as "The Displaced Person" in the *Sewanee Review;* its ending was incorporated without revision into the expanded version.[23]

The two encounters between Mrs. McIntyre and Father Flynn—masterpieces of misunderstood meaning and ignored revelation—expose fully the story's interpretive word concerning displacer and displacement. The conclusion of the story narrating Mrs. McIntyre's fate not only reemphasizes the motif of the spiritual displacement of displacers so evident in Mrs. Shortley's experience, but also, and more significantly, announces the paradoxical pattern of man's redemption. Mr. Guizac, a fictional transfiguration of Jesus, *the* Displaced Person, attempts to restore equality to human relationships by upsetting the unregenerate status quo. The redemptive mode of the physically displaced is to demand that personal values be re-placed in their proper perspectives.

Disturbed obviously by the fact that Mr. Guizac has been uprooted from his country but equally convinced that she cannot consider herself "responsible for all the extra people in the world," Mrs. McIntyre shores up her decision to release him with the words: "He didn't have to come in the first place!" Father Flynn, however, contemplating the Transfiguration of Jesus in the resplendence of the peacock, thinks she is referring to Christ's advent and, always happy for an opportunity to give religious instruction, unintentionally announces the good news of salvation, divine action (Christ) through human cooperation (Mr. Guizac). "He came to redeem us!" he replies.

Their second conversation, after Mr. Shortley's return and the inception of his vocal pogrom against D.P.'s, yields the negative assertion that becomes the story's ultimate affirmation. Once again their concerns are contrapuntal. Unable to see how Father Flynn's theological platitudes about redemption are relevant to her "practical" need to dismiss Mr. Guizac, Mrs. McIntyre glares at the priest fiercely and says, "As far as I'm concerned, . . . Christ was just another D.P." Whereas ambiguity of antecedent alone had linked Christ and Mr. Guizac in the earlier dialogue, the connection is now explicitly made. Insisting that her "obligation is to the people who've done something for their country," she announces, "I'm going to let that man go." Father Flynn himself associates displaced man with Christ as he counsels her not "to turn the porrrr man out": "Think of the thousands of them, think of the ovens and the boxcars and the camps and the sick children and Christ Our Lord." Although there is little ambiguity in Mrs. McIntyre's intention, her complaint, following hard upon Father Flynn's appeal, obviously applies to both Mr. Guizac and Christ in the analogical pattern of their dialogue. "He's extra and he's upset the balance around here," she says. It is the prevailing balance of racial discrimination that Mr. Guizac would have upset; Mrs. McIntyre's rejection of him is clear indication that she is not ready for the radical comm*unity* that redemption entails. In trying to marry his cousin into freedom with the young Negro Sulk, Mr. Guizac was quietly offering to rural Georgia a racially unified society that Mrs. McIntyre and "her class" scorn.

That Mr. Guizac's foreign ways have preserved him from the biases of the American tradition is observed by white and black alike. "You recollect how he shook [the niggers'] hands," Mrs. Shortley had reminded her husband, "like he didn't know the difference, like he might have been as black as them." Astor reflects on Mr. Guizac's

"different ways of doing" in language that anticipates the
tragedy of the rejected redeemer: "It warn't like it was
what he should ought or oughtn't.. .. It was like what
nobody else don't do." Mrs. McIntyre is willing finally—in
the moment of demonic collusion that prevents her, Mr.
Shortley, or Sulk from shouting a warning to Mr.
Guizac—to forego the clear economic advantage that he
offers in order to preserve the ancient taboos. She utterly
misconstrues what "*her* moral obligation . . . to her own
people" actually is. Rejecting the human savior, she
forsakes the very possibility of salvation for herself and her
people. Mrs. McIntyre's displacement from her true country is complete; the isolation of her last days, total and
pathetic. Her first husband, the Judge, had been absolutely
right when he warned, "The devil you know is better than
the devil you don't."

II

In the title story of the second collection, "Everything
That Rises Must Converge," the conflict between mind and
heart is personified in the interaction of Julian and his
mother. The convergence announced by the title takes
place on at least three levels: son against mother, new
generation against old, and race against race. The hermeneutic word of judgment becomes potential conversion for
Julian personally inasmuch as it illumines his existence on
each of these three levels of convergence and as the story
ends he has at least begun running toward the light.

On the most obvious level, Julian, the victim of a
demonic self-sufficiency, necessarily rejects his mother
because he has no faculty for relating to her love, however
imperfect it may be. Julian feels that he has turned out
well in spite of his mother. He considers himself enlightened on the race question; his mother's condescending
attitude appalls him so much that he likes to sit next to
Negroes on the bus "in reparation . . . for his mother's

sins." If "condescension is truly part of her motivation,"[24] as Carter Martin states, and not principally
Julian's warped view of her, her maternal and class
instincts are infinitely superior to her son's outright and
deliberate disdain for anyone lacking his education and
"tolerance." It is quite clear that Julian wants to hurt his
mother more than make amends to God or Negroes, for he
experiences "an evil urge to break her spirit."

Moreover, the exaggerated liberal values of his generation clash violently and inevitably with the gentility and
graciousness of the dying older order. Although "both
Julian and his mother envision the ancestral house as a
focus of yearning," they do not, as Orvell goes on to say,
both imagine it "as an unfallen state."[25] For Julian's
mother it is indeed a reminder of mythical days, but
Julian's visualization of it is more a willing confirmation of
the fall. For him it is a place of isolation from the masses.
It is a materialization of the "mental bubble" that is his
refuge whenever he cannot "bear to be a part of what [is]
going on around him."

The racial convergence takes place on the integrated bus
to the Y, when the Negro woman, caught in the rising tide
of an impatient oppressed minority, lashes out against the
patronizing generosity of the gradualistic majority. There
is a twofold ironic exchange of identity. The black woman
is wearing the very hat that Julian's mother had purchased
in an effort to keep from meeting herself "coming and
going." His mother's "innocence," that "for a moment
Julian had an uncomfortable sense of," apparently preserves her from a recognition of their shared emblem of
human equality: "An amused smile came over her face as
if the woman were a monkey that had stolen her hat." But
there is no question of Julian's realization that he and the
little boy, Carver, have exchanged mothers. Julian and the
Negro woman are obviously related through a bond of
mutual irascibility and impatience, and the fact that the
black woman's attitude is more justifiable does not lessen
their deserved relationship. Carver and Julian's mother, on

the other hand, apparently understand each other as mother and son should since they both have active hearts.

When Julian's mother gives Carver a penny, the Negro woman strikes her with her bulging red pocketbook. Despite the fact that Julian had tried to warn his mother, it is clear that the ugliness of his own antipathy for her has been objectified in the violence of the onslaught. Julian's tragic responsibility for his mother's death had begun with his first deliberate attempt to provoke her, when he left her side to sit next to the Negro across the aisle from them: "He felt his tension suddenly lift as if he had openly declared war on her." From that moment on, her blood pressure, apparent in her "unnaturally red" face, literally rises to the breaking point so that her presumably fatal stroke comes quickly as a lasting tide of reproach and righteous judgment against Julian and his kind.

Julian's desire to spell out the lesson for his mother is changed to sorrow and confusion when the impact of his mother's seizure reaches him. Her heart has been dislodged from its moorings by the force of the blow. As she lumbers pitifully down the street, "with a headlong movement in the wrong direction," she seems unable to determine Julian's identity. She mutters simply that she is going home rather than to the Y. Her last request, the poignant "Tell Caroline to come get me," becomes the grace of judgment as well as conversion for Julian. The extreme irony of her request stems from the fact that, as a possible punishment for her, Julian had "imagined his mother lying desperately ill and his being able to secure only a Negro doctor for her." His mother spontaneously prefers the reassuring presence of her former black maid to the dubious comfort of her "stranger" son. Her single functioning eye, which rakes his face for the last time and finds nothing, implies a judgment even more scathing than her words achieved.

As his mother crumples to the pavement, the horror of his sin breaks upon him like the ominous dawn of a dark day of grief. Julian, in panic, runs down the street for help, but the tide of darkness "seems to sweep him back to her, postponing from moment to moment his entry into the world of guilt and sorrow." We are led to believe that Julian will, indeed, enter that world. Nevertheless, the extent of his sin, measured by the horrifying judgment leveled against him, must necessarily prolong his period of purgation.

The title of the story is taken from Teilhard de Chardin's *The Phenomenon of Man,* and O'Connor doubtlessly used it with respect. Although riddled with irony, the story ultimately yields a fundamentally positive meaning. In each of the areas of conflict, there is a higher level of convergence that reflects the forward thrust of the evolutionary process, however painful and gradual a process "Tell Caroline to come get me" implies. There is no growth, Teilhard explains, without diminishment. Julian's mother dies without solace and only thus wins his love and respect. The request for Caroline triggers his realization that, for all its defects, the older generation had more genuine personal feeling for Negroes than his with its heartless liberalism. And the gratuitous violence of the black woman's action contrasted with the anticipated comforts of a Negro nurse intensifies Julian's painful awakening to the complexity of racial tension. The condescending heart is less dangerous than the martial mind. Though slow perhaps in its adjustment to change, the heart gives a surer sense of ultimate direction than the mind's "principles."

"Greenleaf" is unique among the collected stories in that its principal antagonist is not human. The scrub bull eating away at Mrs. May's substance is an incarnation both of a changing social order and of divine revelation. The use of natural symbolism in support of interpretive human discourse and transcendent revelation is not rare in O'Connor's work, but it is not always integral to the aesthetic unity of the work. The action of the bull in "Greenleaf," however, is so smoothly assimilated into the

inevitable process of social change typified by the Greenleafs and the fictional elements themselves are so carefully
interwoven into the story's hermeneutic pattern that this
may well be O'Connor's most effective use of natural
symbolism.

From the opening description of the bull's "crowned
head" and his listening outside Mrs. May's window "like
some patient god come down to woo her" to his final
embrace in death "like a wild tormented lover," the
textual allusions to the Greenleaf bull as divine lover have
been carefully exposed by the critics. It is the more
mundane significance of the bull that, at least until the
ending of the story, assaults Mrs. May's sensibilities.
Although she must discover whose bull it actually is, the
threat to her security is clear from the outset. Its
destructive presence in her hedge, as "a steady rhythmic
chewing as if something were eating one wall of the
house," even filters through her senses in her sleep. The
bull belongs of course to O. T. and E. T. Greenleaf, who
through their government-financed education, marriage,
housing, and "milk parlor" are about to inherit the
land—from Mrs. May. She dreams that the chewing
continues "through the house, eating her and the boys,
. . . eating everything until nothing was left but the
Greenleafs on a little island all their own in the middle of
what had been her place." But at the story's conclusion
the Greenleaf bull has "eaten" only Mrs. May; she alone is
responsible for hastening the capitulation of the Mays to
the advancing order of Greenleafs. She has had her
property entailed so that her sons could not leave it to
their wives if they married (she was convinced that as soon
as she died they would "marry trash and bring it in here
and ruin everything"), for Wesley and Scofield had already
proven to her that "neither of *them* cared what happened
to the place" (my emphasis).

Descriptive emphasis on sound and sharp dialogical
exchanges support the hermeneutical role of language in
the story. Sound is either so diminished that it requires

strained attention or so loud that it is deafening; the
emphasis throughout is on the importance of *listening*. The
story's first image is of the bull standing below Mrs. May's
bedroom window in the moonlight with "his head raised as
if he listened . . . for a stir inside the room." When the
clouds hide the moon, there is nothing to mark the bull's
presence "but the sound of steady chewing." Twice in her
sleep Mrs. May is conscious of sounds, first of the "steady
rhythmic chewing," later of "the sun trying to burn
through the tree line . . . as if some large stone were
grinding a hole on the outside wall of her brain"; then the
sun changes in appearance from "a swollen red ball" into
"a bullet" bursting through the trees. At the prophetic
moment when Mrs. May discovers the pentecostal Mrs.
Greenleaf in the embarrassing act of praying, "the sound
was so piercing that [Mrs. May] felt as if some violent
unleashed force had broken out of the ground and was
charging toward her"—an image that establishes the link
between Mrs. Greenleaf's prayer and the bull's lethal
embrace. And in the understated conclusion of the story
Mrs. May's seeming to "whisper" into the animal's ear
suggests the necessity, if not the desirability, of straining
to hear reality's revelation.

The war of words between Mrs. May and Mr. Greenleaf
demonstrates how one who must invariably have the last
word is fittingly judged by the sharp retorts of her own
proud tongue. Responding to Mr. Greenleaf's annoying
comment, "If hit was my boys, they would have got thet
bull up theirself," Mrs. May says, "If your boys had any
pride, Mr. Greenleaf, . . . there are many things that they
would not *allow* their mother to do." When Mr. Greenleaf
drawls, "I thank Gawd for ever-thang," Mrs. May imagines
her response: "You might as well, . . . you've never done
anything for yourself." There is of course nothing that
Wesley and Scofield will not allow her to do, nor any
justifiable reason for divorcing faith and works.

Mrs. May predictably pronounces her own last judgment
(and ours) while Mrs. Greenleaf's prayer prophetically

foreshadows the manner of Mrs. May's death. When Mrs. Greenleaf shrieks, "Oh, Jesus, stab me in the heart!" while seeming to embrace the ground, her fundamentalist piety begs for the grace of healing. It is Mrs. May, however, who experiences the literal answer to that prayer when her heart is pierced by one of the bull's horns and embraced by the other. In reacting to Mrs. Greenleaf's pentecostal excesses, Mrs. May had tactlessly reminded Mr. Greenleaf, "Everything in moderation, you know"—an admonition she would have done well to have remembered when she launched her monomaniacal campaign against the Greenleaf bull. She is the victim of the bull's irresistible attraction to cars, but more precisely of her own refusal to allow anyone or anything—even history and least of all God—to alter her view of reality.

The ending of "Greenleaf" continues to be a source of critical debate. Among the major critics Carter Martin and Miles Orvell tend to overinterpret apparently on the assumption that meaning within the story and therefore for the reader is necessarily *accepted* revelation for the protagonist. Martin concludes that "Mrs. May comes to understand the injustice of the world as an aspect of the condition of man, not as a personal affront,"[26] while Orvell suggests that "despite the horrible image of a woman impaled on the horns of a dying beast, one also feels that this is a 'happy' ending: the persistent suitor has at last gained his mark."[27] But from the point of view of the New Hermeneutic, even though the word's proffered illumination of existence constitutes the meaning of the piece, the offer itself does not compel response. Although the seeming injustice of the world certainly relates to the story's meaning, there is little evidence in the text for asserting that Mrs. May "comes to understand" it that specifically; nor is it reasonable to project "a 'happy' ending" from the tone of the love imagery.

The revelation that assaults Mrs. May is diametrically opposed to her own hypocritical philosophy of moderation. Three descriptive phrases have bearing on our judgment of her reaction. As if to exaggerate the burden of that revelation, O'Connor saves the disclosure of Mrs. May's extreme self-reliance for the instant before she is united with her nemesis. As she waits in the pasture for Mr. Greenleaf to return, she reflects: "Before any kind of judgment seat, she would be able to say: I've worked, I have not wallowed." When she realizes that it is the bull, not Mr. Greenleaf, "racing toward her," she remains still, "not in fright, but in a freezing *unbelief*." Gored by the bull, "she had the look of a person whose sight had been suddenly restored but *who finds the light unbearable*." Finally, when Mr. Greenleaf reached her, "she *seemed* . . . to be bent over whispering some last discovery into the animal's ear" (my emphases throughout). If the conclusion does not grant Mrs. May the grace of an affirmative response, it leaves little doubt that she has at least received the "unbearable" message.

Mrs. May stands condemned most precisely by the indictment that she had wanted to shout at her shiftless sons, "You'll find out one of these days, you'll find out what *Reality* is when it's too late!" She at least finds out "what *Reality* is" even if it is too late. And what was undoubtedly her rashest and saddest miscalculation was formulated by her own "defiant" inner voice: "I'll die when I get good and ready." The structure of reality is certainly not determined by the works and attitudes of man.

Of all of O'Connor's stories, "A View of the Woods" most obviously demands either a mythic or an allegorical interpretation. Even after close scrutiny it lacks the apparent strength of interpretive language in the resolution of its dramatic conflict that is characteristic of her mature parables. Like Jesus' parable of the Sower, which the synoptic evangelists unanimously allegorize, the conflict between Mark Fortune and Mary Fortune Pitts easily yields to allegorical interpretation. The Edenic allusions too are potent enough to recommend a Judaeo-Christian mythic explanation; Miles Orvell, for instance, suggests "that the land the old man seeks to destroy in his dream is a kind of Edenic paradise, and that the process he has set in motion under the name of progress is the Fall."[28] Yet even if allegory and myth are the obvious servants of meaning here, interpretive language is present to each of these modes; there is, moreover, sufficient indication of the historical particularity that the parable in the strict sense calls for.

Because of his refusal to see his land as anything but material to be abused in the name of artificial lakes and fishing clubs, supermarkets and drive-in theaters, Mark Fortune is caught up in "the rattle of everything that [leads] to the future." Not only is progress itself serpentine, but also the man through whose collusion the lot in front of the Fortune home will be converted into a gas station. Tilman, whom Mary Fortune sniffs as if scenting "an enemy," is clearly the tempter from the garden: "He sat habitually with his arms folded on the counter and his insignificant head weaving snake-fashion above them. He had a triangular-shaped face with the point at the bottom and the top of his skull was covered with a cap of freckles. His eyes were green and very narrow and his tongue was always exposed in his partly opened mouth." Such a zoologically accurate description as this seems to point to an Edenic charade with the same obtrusive precision that the highway sign "Here it is, Friends, TILMAN'S!" pinpoints the demon's "dark store." The name itself reminds us that his function is to till mankind under the earth.

The latter-day Adam and Eve are the improbable seventy-nine year old Mark Fortune and his nine year old granddaughter Mary Fortune Pitts. It is undoubtedly O'Connor's deliberate variation on Genesis to have the *man* succumb to Satan's ruse. Chauvinist male that he is, Mark Fortune is convinced that Mary, unlike his other deplorable offspring, is enough like him to have been made "bone from his bone." Her face is "a small replica of the old man's," and "the spiritual distance between them [is] slight," or so the pseudopatriarch thinks. Although Mary Fortune's maniacal tenacity of purpose is recognizably— and tragically—cut from one of the old man's ribs, there is little else in her spiritual makeup that suggests "his unmistakable likeness"; their attitudes toward the land are diametrically opposed. For Mary Fortune the lot in front of the house possesses practical, aesthetic, and mystical meaning, and even its practical aspects for her are infinitely superior to Mr. Fortune's crass materialism. It is pasture for her father's calves as well as playground for the children; more significantly it functions aesthetically as "lawn" and mystically as "a view of the woods." O'Connor's farcical variation on the story of the fall absolves woman from the complete spiritual blindness that mistakes stewardship for absolute dominion, while acknowledging sufficient temperamental likeness between old man and child to sustain the myth's tragic conclusion—expulsion from the garden is indeed a kind of death.

The "frequent little verbal tilts" that they have, which Mr. Fortune considers "a sport like putting a mirror up in the front of a rooster and watching him fight his reflection," lead to a climactic exchange with the sting of mutual final judgment. The turning point in their titanic physical struggle comes when Mr. Fortune looks "into his own image" and hears it say, "You been whipped . . . by me, . . . and I'm PURE Pitts." Typical of man's refusal to accept responsibility for his image, especially the child of his sin whatever form it may take, the old man responds vehemently, "There's not an ounce of Pitts in me." Their denial of a common heredity is a ludicrous variation on the moral irresponsibility of Adam after the fall. The man tells God, "The woman you gave me for a companion, she gave me fruit from the tree and I ate it," and when the Lord God pursues his inquiry with the woman, asking, "What is this that you have done?" she blames the serpent, "The serpent tricked me, and I ate" (Gen. 3:12–13). For on the mythic level there is no way that Mr. Fortune can deny his kinship with the Pittses, or Mary Fortune Pitts hers with the Fortunes.

When Mr. Fortune destroys the child of his perverse stubbornness, the violence of his self-denial is sufficient to cause his own death. As the story ends he is flat on his back, trapped by the very woods he was willing to sacrifice to progress.[29] There is no one to help him, only a clay-gorging yellow monster; the trees alone create the illusion of freedom of movement, but they are oblivious to his plight: "The gaunt trees had thickened into mysterious dark files that were marching across the water and away into the distance."

The equally persistent allegorical reading interprets the conflict between "PURE Pitts" and "PURE Fortune," machine and woods, as the perennial historical clash between Progress and Tradition. There is of course no predictable outcome to their convergence, although O'Connor typically leaves us with no doubt where her own sympathies lie. The protagonists' claims to be "PURE Fortune" and "PURE Pitts" are taken as accurate assessments of their respective disdain and veneration for the lot as "view." And although Progress destroys Tradition, Pittses will inherit the land as a result of Mary's liberating death. In a twofold way Mary Fortune upholds tradition by putting her life on the line: she will let no man but her father discipline her, and she will not sacrifice the transcendence of view for the tacky conveniences of modernity. Her final pronouncement of independence of her grandfather is supported by nature's refusal to comfort the dying old man. The only view of the woods Mark Fortune is granted is of a trap formed by dark, gaunt trees.

As parable in the strict sense, "A View of the Woods" illumines the bonds of human solidarity and instructs us to beware of the enduring human tendency to make others over into our own image. The tragedy of Mr. Fortune's isolation is that he needs companionship so badly he dares to confuse physical similarities with complete spiritual kinship. Even though the story obviously does not deny the possibility of spiritual affinity, it plainly acknowledges the tragedy inherent in attempting to impose rather than discover bonds.

In "The Enduring Chill," Asbury is returning home to Timberboro to die, or so he thinks. His redeeming feature is undoubtedly the fact that he is taking at least death seriously. He is not prepared, as his friend Goetz in New York had urged, "to see it all as illusion." He is convinced that death is "coming to him legitimately, as a justification, as a gift from life." Even though "he had failed his god, Art, he had nevertheless been its faithful servant," and so he believes "Art [is] sending him Death." Asbury has so romanticized his projected escape from inadequacy that the personification of his god appears in his dream alongside the verifiable "lean dark figure in a Roman collar." Death will be "his greatest triumph" because he will use it as an occasion to introduce his mother to reality. The Kafkaesque letter that he has written for her benefit and that will be given to her only after his death will assist her, he hopes, "in the process of growing up," if the experience does not kill her first.

As a foretaste of the displeasure that his mother will experience in reading his letter, Asbury insists that she send for a nearby Jesuit priest, knowing that his request will offend her traditionalist views. "He would talk to a man of culture before he died—even in this desert!" He hopes that the neighboring priest will be "a trifle more worldly perhaps, a trifle more cynical" than Ignatius Vogle, the sophisticated young Jesuit he had met in New York. Instead, Asbury is visited by Father Finn, a "massive" old man, deaf in one ear and blind in one eye, who is concerned about whether Asbury is saying his morning and night prayers, whether he has any "trouble with purity," whether he knows his catechism. Asbury responds with a series of agnostic declarations; there is clearly no meeting of minds. In response to Father Finn's insistence that he "pray regularly," Asbury shouts that

"the myth of the dying god has always fascinated [him] ."
God is after all "an idea created by man"; moreover, the
artist, he insists, "prays by creating." Father Finn assures
Asbury that there is still hope for his salvation, since he is
not dead yet; but he must ask God "to send the Holy
Ghost." Asbury says furiously, "The Holy Ghost is the last
thing I'm looking for!" "He may be the last thing you get"
is the priest's illuminating response. Before leaving Asbury,
Father Finn, one of the Gospel "babes" to whom
revelation is given in place of the "learned and wise,"
completes his judgment of the sick writer: "The Holy
Ghost will not come until you see yourself as you are—a
lazy ignorant conceited youth!"

The day after this depressing interview, Asbury feels "as
if he were a shell that had to be filled with something but
he did not know what"; he concludes that he needs "some
last significant culminating experience that he must make
for himself before he [dies]—make for himself out of his
own intelligence," because he has "always relied on
himself and . . . never been a sniveler after the ineffable."
His last attempt to redeem the time, unlike his first the
summer before, is simply ineffectual; the previous summer's "moment of communion" was the cause of his
illness. Wanting to "smoke together one last time," he calls
for the black farm hands Randall and Morgan, but they
merely pocket the packages of cigarettes, commenting how
Asbury "certly does look well." The summer before
Asbury had smoked with them in the barn and ruined two
cans of milk as a result; but when he poured the
communion cup of unpasteurized milk, only they were
smart enough not to drink it. The illness which he thought
was unto death is undulant fever. "It'll keep coming back
but it won't kill you!" his mother announces happily.

Robbed of the easy but dramatic escape of death and
the opportunity to give the letter to his mother from the
protected distance of the grave, Asbury is left to himself
and his problems—and to the presence of the "fierce bird
with spread wings," formed by the water stains on the

ceiling of his bedroom. "An icicle crosswise in its beak," the bird—which often gave the illusion of being in motion and about to descend mysteriously—had been with him throughout his life, from childhood on, but especially during his illness as he lay gazing at the ceiling. Now the "purifying terror" of its descent coincides with the recurring waves of the chill that grip his body. He knows that for the rest of his life he will be visited regularly by the salutary realization of the futility of self-reliance. The last film of illusion is stripped from his eyes "as if by a whirlwind." Death will not spare him the agony of rebirth to new life. Father Finn's prophetic judgment has come to literal fulfillment, as well as Father Vogle's more cautious assertion that "there is a real probability of the New Man, assisted, of course, . . . by the Third Person of the Trinity." The last thing Asbury wanted is, providentially, the last thing he gets—the implacable descent of the chastening Spirit "emblazoned in ice instead of fire." The Holy Ghost, whom Scripture calls the Spirit of Truth, reveals to Asbury and the reader the icy warning that the fate of the self-made savior may seem worse than death.

The protagonist in "The Comforts of Home" is a historian and a scholar, president of the local historical society, who is writing about the first settlers in his county. Thomas is interested in origins. Although the devil is "just a manner of speaking for him," he knows that he can prove to his mother "from early Christian history that no excess of virtue is justified, that a moderation of good produces likewise a moderation in evil, that if Anthony of Egypt had stayed at home and attended to his sister, no devils would have plagued him." Virtue in moderation is, for Thomas, "the principle of order and the only thing that makes life bearable." He sees himself as the perfect blend of his father and mother because he thinks that "he inherited his father's reason without his ruthlessness and his mother's love of good without her tendency to pursue it."

It is apparently his mother's excessive love for him that leads her so often to do "the *nice thing*" for others, especially those less fortunate than they. ("Taking a box of candy was her favorite nice thing to do.") When Thomas objects vehemently to her letting the young psychopath Sarah Ham remain in their house, his mother responds characteristically, "I keep thinking it might be you." Earlier when Thomas had complained about Sarah's criminal activity, his mother had answered, "You don't know what you'd do in a pinch," and her words are clearly prophetic. Although Thomas protests that he knows at least that he "wouldn't pass a bad check," his mother's practical wisdom is obviously superior to his ivory-towerish intellectualism. It was at times such as these that "he could not endure her love for him. . . . When virtue got out of hand with her a sense of devils grew upon him."

In his exasperation over the threat to his privacy that Sarah poses, Thomas wonders what the attitude of God would be in a situation like this, "meaning if possible to adopt it." At these times, too, Thomas "truly mourned the death of his father though he had not been able to endure him in life," for his father "would have put his foot down." So he allows his father—in the absence of God—to take up "a squatting position in his mind." A historian of origins should have known that "squatters" have no title to the place they settle in, least of all to another's mind. Suggestions for disposing of Sarah enter his mind, and their "moral tone indicated that they had come from a mind akin to his father's." Thomas nevertheless allows his father to take control of his paralyzed will, even though (until the end) he undoubtedly likes to think that he is translating his father's ruthlessness into the terms of his own moderation; a dishonest plan for having Sarah put away is supposedly "below his moral stature."

Victim of the inner evil that he has dallied with, Thomas lies about the gun he has placed in Sarah's purse in anticipation of the sheriff's arrival and the tone of his voice is unmistakably his father's. "I found it in her bag," he shouts, "the dirty criminal slut stole my gun." Sarah's retort is a brief but definitive word of judgment: "Found it my eye!" When Thomas fires his gun, the blast ironically is "like a sound meant to bring an end to evil in the world. Thomas heard it as a sound that would shatter the laughter of sluts until all shrieks were stilled and nothing was left to disturb the peace of perfect order." Instead of putting an end to evil, Thomas's connivance with evil has merely contributed to its control over his world.[30] The only interpretation that we are given of the final scene comes from the malignant mind of Sheriff Farebrother, who is "another edition of Thomas's father." The scene that confronts him meets for once the expectations of his "nasty" mind. It is clear to Farebrother that "the killer and the slut were about to collapse into each other's arms" over the body of Thomas's mother. Thomas's last condition is worse than his first. In trying to shut the door on a questionable demon, he has let in two very real ones—his father and Farebrother; he has confused the appearance of evil with its reality. Thomas, now, is clearly worse than his father, who by gesture alone had lived his lie, never deigning to tell one. And the evil that is in Thomas's heart is far worse than the evil he sought to extinguish because he, unlike Sarah, is responsible for his act.

Although language offers its clearest hermeneutic warning early in the story in Thomas's mother's practical caveat "You don't know what you'd do in a pinch," it is only when joined to Sarah's final accusation, the last words spoken—"Found it my eye!"—that word approximates meaning in the story. Judgment is linked significantly to vision. Thomas should have had sufficient insight to realize that his father had no more right over the sanctity of the human spirit than he had in deceitfully placing his gun in Sarah's bag. "The Comforts of Home" offers a variation on the motif of "A Good Man Is Hard to Find"; it insists that the eschatological crisis reveals what we are essentially while inverting that story's ultimate disclosure. Thomas professes moderation, yet discovers "in a pinch" his deep inner inclination to vice rather than virtue. He claims knowledge of origins yet overlooks the origin of his personal sin in first yielding to the known influence of malignancy. The "sense of devils" that Thomas had experienced in the presence of his mother's incursions into virtue was actually an ignored though genuine rumor of his own demonic ruthlessness.

Even if Sarah's approach to Thomas is consistently and humorously drawn in sexual terms, it is hard to understand fully how Orvell can read the tale as "a criticism of the kind of self-deception that sees sexuality as the enemy of Christian love."[31] Insofar as Sarah's offensive "psychopathic personality" is described from Thomas's point of view, it is really his bookishness and dependence upon mother that is being parodied through the sexual references. It is not sexuality as such that makes Thomas cringe, but sexual license, perhaps genuine nymphomania. The mother's attitude is indeed a caricature of Christian love, but the story is Thomas's and its "uncommonly complicated moral satire"[32] broadsides the more universal human error of using unquestionably evil means to achieve a dubious good.

"The Lame Shall Enter First" is the only one of O'Connor's stories in which the pruning word spoken to the protagonist is also its title. There are, actually, two significant levels to the dramatic conflict in the story: the principal struggle between Sheppard and Rufus is resolved in the evangelical saying of the title; the minor war between them for mastery of Norton, though never formally declared, is terminated by a related pronouncement. When Rufus screeches at Sheppard, "The lame'll carry off the prey!" it is clear to the reader, if not yet to Sheppard, that Rufus had prevailed in the contest over Norton's spirit; but when Rufus screams "The lame shall enter first!" at the vanquished Sheppard, there can be no doubt that freedom has won another victory over psychological determinism.

Although the possibility generated by the word is by its nature ever open, of structural necessity the end of a story limits the period of grace for the protagonist. If Sheppard's metanoia is no more than appearance, as I hope to demonstrate, the word spoken to him is judgment only; to discuss possibility for a protagonist beyond the evidence of the story's conclusion is at best overinterpretation, if not outright misinterpretation. In "The Lame Shall Enter First" an underlying pattern of deepening denial and solemn abjuration of responsibility suggests Sheppard's gradual disintegration rather than his improvement. Whether or not these are evangelical allusions to Peter's denial and Pilate's repudiation of Jesus, the threefold repetition itself is solemn enough to vouch for the extremity of the context. In successive stages of Sheppard's dealings with the police, each reaction of his represents a deterioration of his relationship with Rufus, and Rufus at least knows it. Sheppard's responses go from honest denial of trust for the sake of salutary punishment, to trust seeking the assurance of an alibi, and ultimately to a lie masking as foolishly misplaced confidence. When the police and Rufus appear finally to tell Sheppard what everyone else has known all along—that Rufus has deliberately perpetrated all the crimes and then planned his own arrest—Sheppard washes his hands of all responsibility in the solemn thrice-repeated formula, "I have nothing to reproach myself with."

An integral reading of the conclusion of the story simply cannot bear the weight of tragic recognition that Charles M. Hegarty proposes.[33] There are, first of all, four apocalyptic images toward the end of the story that project an expectation of judgment rather than purgation. As Rufus leaves the house after eating the pages from the stolen Bible, he pauses at the door, "a small black figure on the threshold of some dark apocalypse." The siren of the police car that Sheppard knows is bringing Rufus back is "like the first shrill note of a disaster warning." Sheppard's reaction to the siren's subsiding moan places him unmistakably in the sixth Bolgia of the *Inferno's* eighth circle (Canto XXIII) where the Pharisees suffer at last from the burdens that they have self-righteously inflicted on others: "He felt a cold weight on his shoulders as if an icy cloak had been thrown about him." It is curious, if not conclusive, that the only impression that the final paragraph gives us of Sheppard's reaction to Norton's suicide completes the Dantean allusion: ". . . at the top [he] reeled back like a man on the edge of a pit."

More significantly, the description itself of Sheppard's supposed "change of heart" reveals an undiminished messianism: only its object is restricted. What Sheppard proposes to do now for Norton is characterized by the same rash dependence on self and self-righteous exaggeration: *"He* would make *everything* up to him. *He* would *never* let him suffer again. *He* would be mother *and* father. He jumped up and ran to his room, to kiss him, to tell him that *he* loved him, that *he* would *never* fail him again" (my emphases).[34] If anything, the new "good shepherd" is more insidiously presumptive than the former, who had only these ambitions for Rufus: "He wanted to give the boy something to reach for besides his neighbor's goods. He wanted to stretch his horizons. He wanted him to *see* the universe, to see that the darkest parts of it could be penetrated." And the sole evidence for Hegarty's "light that purges as it illuminates" would seem to be the bulb in Norton's empty bedroom.

Rufus's exclamations—"The lame shall enter first!" and "The lame'll carry off the prey!"—imitate the triumphant note of the Gospel beatitudes, condemning Sheppard for his clinical positivism that denies the mysteries of freedom and evil in the world, while reminding us once again that "Jesus thown everything off balance." A world in which mischief is merely a compensation for lameness is Sheppard's pitiable illusion; Rufus knows that genuine salvation has nothing to do with orthopedic shoes. Sheppard's psychological clarity about the source of Rufus's problem is based oddly enough on what seems to be the primitive superstition that physical deformity is linked to "evil," and Rufus wisely will have none of it. In response to Norton's early insistence that his father is "good" because "he helps people," Rufus offers the story's fundamental optic for judging the effectiveness of human endeavor, "I don't care if he's good or not. He ain't *right*!" Goodness without vision is at best irrelevant. It is Rufus, therefore, who provides Norton with the belief that he so much needs—that his mother has somehow survived death—since his mother alone apparently had shown him the love that his "big tin Jesus" father could never offer.

Ruby Turpin's dramatic conflict in "Revelation," as I proposed briefly in chapter 1, is a prototype of the hermeneutic structure of Flannery O'Connor's stories. If the title of the story were not sufficient indication, Ruby herself—"a respectable, hardworking, church-going woman"—is portrayed as being immediately certain about the source of, if not the reason for, her encounter with the young psychology major in the doctor's waiting room. She is dumbfounded that "she had been singled out for *the message*, though there was trash in the room to whom it might justly have been applied" (my emphasis). The ultimate cause of the power of the human word that interprets the lives of O'Connor's protagonists, though explicit here, is always at least by implication divine. The root meaning of "revelation" is "to draw back the veil"; thus the New Testament Book of Revelation claims to disclose the ultimate mystery of God's plan operating in the world. It is appropriate that the only story of O'Connor's that lays bare the religious dynamics of her hermeneutic core is itself called "Revelation"—an observation that contributes some additional support, I think, to Forrest Ingram's thesis that the cycle of stories in the second collection properly ends with this one.[35] As reassuring as this unveiling may be, the essential point that I have been trying to make remains true: the hermeneutic structure stands dramatically as a saving dialogue *among men*: it nevertheless illumines existence at its very core. Such is the effect of O'Connor's tales analogous to the parables of Jesus.

Characteristic of the exposed dynamism of the story is the blatantly indicative name given to the Wellesley girl, reading the "thick blue book . . . entitled *Human Development*" and listening painfully to Mrs. Turpin's social commentary. What is unexpected is that Mary Grace, a fat, ugly girl, "blue with acne," is a budding intellectual—utterly unique in Flannery O'Connor's world where intellectuals are typically judged by others, rather than the ones judging. When she throws the book at Ruby and sinks her fingers quickly into Ruby's neck, the latter is jolted violently from the secure moorings of her social hierarchy and forced to reassess her vision. Mary Grace whispers the word of revelation to the dazed Ruby Turpin: "Go back to hell where you came from, you old wart hog!" Then the deranged girl is carried away quickly by ambulance to a hospital.

By external standards Ruby is a "good" woman, "grateful" to God for all her material blessings and her "good disposition" and trying "to help anybody out that [needs] it," yet she tends to take back with her mind what her hands have offered. Even though she does help "trashy" people, she is convinced deep down of the futility of it: "Help them you must, but help them you couldn't." She is grateful for what she has, but her sense of dependence has not prevented her from thinking "that you had to *have* certain things before you could *know* certain things." Her stratification of society on the basis of possessions has placed her precariously close to the top. She occupies herself at night "naming the classes of people": "On the bottom of the heap were most colored people, not the kind she would have been if she had been one, but most of them; then next to them—not above, just away from—were the white-trash; then above them were the home-owners, and above them the home-and-land-owners, to which she and Claud belonged. Above she and

Claud were people with a lot of money and much bigger houses and much more land."

Despite the onslaught of grace, Ruby begrudges every inch of self she must yield to reevaluation. While taking out her wrath on her pigs with the spray from a hose, she directs her questions with the fury of a latter-day Job at the acknowledged source of the revelation: "How am I a hog and me both? . . . How am I a hog? . . . Exactly how am I like them?"[36] The answer comes back to Ruby in the form of a double vision. "As if through the very heart of mystery," she looks down into the pig parlor where the frightened hogs have settled in one corner, seeming "to pant with a secret life." Then, turning to the sunset, she sees a purple streak in the sky, an extension of the nearby highway, as "a vast swinging bridge extending upward from the earth through a field of living fire," on which "a vast horde of souls were rumbling toward heaven." The "life-giving knowledge" that identification with hogs, even her clean ones, has brought her is projected onto the sunset. Ruby realizes that the actual order of salvation has nothing to do with possessions, because at the head of the procession are "whole companies of white-trash, clean for the first time in their lives," and bringing up the rear are people like herself and Claud, who own a home and some land. She can see "by their shocked and altered faces that even their virtues [are] being burned away." Those who exalt themselves will indeed be humbled. As she returns to the house, the new vision of reality is firmly planted in her mind, replacing the old order that she had so carefully but foolishly constructed. Ruby Turpin truly believes now that the first will be last and the last first.[37]

Ruby has allowed herself to be cut down to size by the word. The story is artfully framed by images of her in relation to the world that confirm her acceptance of the revelation. Our first impression of Ruby is of a "very large" woman "looming" over the other patients in a ridiculously small waiting room; she "[makes] it look even smaller by her presence." At the end of the story, Ruby is

alone, "bent" over the side of her pig pen, staring into the
heart of mystery, dwarfed by the cosmic dimensions of the
apocalyptic sunset. Moreover, Ruby's ability to classify
people by looking at their feet is ironic foreshadowing of
her realization of her actual level in creation's order. And
the very cause of her pride in possessions—the immaculate
pig parlor—suggests a biblical indictment of her as "un-
clean" of heart. The meaning of the story is more precise
therefore than Carter Martin implies when he appropriates
in this context Robert Drake's general comment about
O'Connor's world ("There is, finally, no salvation in
works, whatever form they may take, or in *self*").[38] Ruby
Turpin did not think either who she was or what she did
would be her salvation; like the servant who received one
talent, she unhappily confused what she was given with her
final reward.

In "Parker's Back," the vagrant protagonist has deserted
not only his home but also, tragically, himself; events
conspire with prophetic insistence to drive Parker back to
his true identity. As a parable about conversion—the word
itself means "a turning round"—it dramatizes the spiritual
process in terms of O. E. Parker's response to the piercing
eyes of the Byzantine Christ in the tattooist's book that
say unequivocally, "GO BACK." The title's literal reference is to Parker's anatomical back that bears the stern
reminder he has wandered from the source; its special
meaning, though, is that "Parker is back," for by the end
of the story he is back from his wanderings, he is back
with Sarah Ruth—because he went back to the image
"with all-demanding eyes"—but on the deepest level he is
back to the use of his own name. The given name that he is
embarrassed by—Obadiah Elihue—is also actually his call.
"Parker's Back" is built on the assumption that the name
is more than an extrinsic attachment to the person; the
name *is* the man, it projects the destiny he is created for.
    Melvin J. Friedman's contention that "the tone of
Biblical pastiche"[39] is apparent throughout "Parker's

Back" is a critical opinion that persists even though it is not always clear, as in Friedman's essay, how "pastiche" is to be taken. O'Connor has borrowed so freely from pertinent biblical narratives that despite the immediate attractiveness of the material she has shaped, the feeling can understandably remain that "Parker's Back" is indeed a hodge-podge of allusions. They include the burning tree and removed shoes from the Moses story, the threefold call of the prophet Samuel, and the desolation of the pecan tree suggesting both the juniper of Elijah and the gourd plant of Jonah; in addition to the appropriated narratives, we have the names themselves, Obadiah Elihue and Sarah Ruth. Yet a close examination of the context of these references indicates that O'Connor's apparent patchwork coalesces neatly the way Parker's nondescript spider-web soul becomes a "perfect arabesque of colors, a garden of trees and birds and beasts." It is only through the subtle pattern of biblical allusions that Parker's unique identity as Obadiah Elihue takes definitive shape.

The precise point of convergence of the biblical narratives is hermeneutic; the names support interpretive meaning inasmuch as the dramatic conflict between Parker and his wife is emblematic of the struggle between the soul and belief. Sarah and Ruth are biblical names associated with disbelief; each was instrumental in a return to origins. Sarah laughed at the promise of a son to Abraham because of her barrenness, yet was the occasion of renewed faith for Abraham (and herself) when the Lord gave them Isaac. Ruth was a Moabite maiden who converted to Yahwism; her mother-in-law Naomi attributes Ruth's faithful companionship on the return to Bethlehem directly to the Lord's favor. Sarah was the ancestress of Israel, Ruth of David; both are in the genealogical line of the Messiah. And Parker's destiny implied in the name Sarah Ruth makes him accept once and for all is, as we shall see, decidedly redemptive.

Each of the prophets referred to, moreover, received commands from the Lord to "GO BACK." Because the

place of the burning bush was sacred, the Lord instructed
Moses to remove his sandals before approaching (Exod.
3:5); it is during the Midian epiphany that the Lord
commissions Moses to liberate His people from bondage in
Egypt: "Go back to Egypt, for all those who wished to kill
you are dead" (Exod. 4:19). Preoccupied with "a suitable
design for his back," the distracted Parker drives his
employer's tractor into a tree; his exclamation "GOD
ABOVE" is more prophetic than blasphemous. Thrown
from the tractor Parker sees "his shoes, quickly being
eaten by the fire."

Samuel, in the Lord's service under Eli, is called three
times before he understands the divine source of the
summons (1 Sam. 3:1–10). Samuel's first prophetic
mission is to "GO BACK" to his master Eli "to tell him
that [the Lord's] judgment on his house shall stand
forever because he knew of his sons' blasphemies against
God and did not rebuke them" (1 Sam. 3:13). In response
to the "voice from inside" that has asked Parker for the
third and last time "Who's there?"—"there was a quality
about it now that seemed final"—he freely uses his full
Christian name and acknowledges in principle the "servant" role that it entails.

The final image of Parker "leaning against the [pecan]
tree, crying like a baby," could refer either to Elijah,
fleeing the wrath of Jezebel and despairing under the
broom tree (formerly "juniper," 1 Kings 19:4), or to
Jonah mourning the death of his gourd plant (Jon. 4:8).
Elijah must anoint a new king for Israel; the Lord tells
him, "Go back by way of the wilderness of Damascus" (1
Kings 19:15). It is more likely though that O'Connor had
the Book of Jonah in mind; not only is there a shared
humor in the two works, but also a patent similarity in
structure. Both are stories about vain attempts to escape
the divine call. Jonah, called to preach repentance to the
Ninevites, boards a ship in Joppa destined for Tarshish
(Spain?). Although Jonah does not literally have to "GO
BACK" to Nineveh—he never attempted to go there in the

first place—he is told by the Lord after the "great fish"
spews him up on dry land, "Go now and denounce
[Nineveh] in the words I gave you" (Jon. 3:2). Like
Jonah, Parker must eventually, even if tearfully, admit the
inevitability of his fate and accept the action of mercy.

It is not surprising that O'Connor should have labored
over the three principal images in the resolution of her
narrative: the configuration of the sunset, Parker's experience of transformation, and the description of the new
man. She wanted the sunset to remind Parker of his
experience with the burning tree; its sudden explosion over
the skyline forces him to "GO BACK" in memory to the
original stimulus toward conversion. Through at least five
revisions we can trace the description of the sunset from a
"tree of fire" to the final "tree of light." More significant
still is her effort to capture the force of its suddenness that
will pin O. E. to the door; O'Connor experimented with
"emerges" and with four variations of "slowly majestically
ascending" before deciding that it must "burst over the
skyline."[40]

The reworking of the transformation metaphor was even
more extensive. There is evidence in the O'Connor
Collection at Milledgeville of at least six variations that
place the transformation *before* Parker gives his name. It is
more precise theologically to have it follow his act of
self-identification, as in the final version of the passage.[41]
Conversion is a rebirth to spiritual innocence; Parker's
inner transformation is appropriately experienced as an
Edenic harmonization of the tattoos on his body.

The story's final sentence was revised at least five times
before the appearance of the clause emphatically repeating
Parker's full Christian name—"who called himself Obadiah
Elihue."[42] The descriptive phrase "crying like a baby,"
found in four of the five MSS and preserved in the
published version, supports the symbolism of Parker's
return to origins, the motif of new life linked to
conversion as in Jesus' reminder to Nicodemus, "Unless a
man has been born over again he cannot see the kingdom

of God" (John 3:3). The repetition of Parker's Christian name completes the baptismal symbolism of rebirth corresponding to the story's hermeneutic demand that Parker "GO BACK" to the call given him in the beginning.

Naming is the most fundamental property of language. Going back to his given name implies an inchoate acceptance of his mission as servant of the one whose image he bears. Parker's sense of wonder is linked inexorably and sanely with body; Sarah Ruth's insistence that God "don't *look*" and her vehement rejection of Parker's religious confession—the implications of which he can scarcely begin to grasp even at the end of the story—epitomize the blindness of disbelief and the violence that members of the kingdom must suffer. The denial that God truly became man is an error as old as the Christian church itself; John the Evangelist wrote his Gospel in answer to its earliest manifestation, the Docetist heresy. The vocation conferred by Parker's name is both cross and glory, for Obadiah Elihue means "the servant of Yahweh, he is God." To be rejected in an act of selfless love, however confused its motivation may have been—the image on his back is after all for Sarah Ruth alone—is to live unmistakably in the likeness of Yahweh's servant. Parker has indeed come back to himself.

Befitting its position at the zenith of O'Connor's career and as the last of her stories to be submitted for publication,[43] "Judgement Day" is a parable about an exile's return to his homeland. Imprisoned in his daughter's New York apartment, Tanner wants to return to Corinth, Georgia at any cost, "dead or alive"; he is willing to pay the price because he knows the tragic shape of his own personal mistake in originally consenting to leave home. His climactic encounter with the black actor, ironically both Judgment Day and Homecoming for him, is the inexorable consequence of the avoided conflict with Dr. Foley, that earlier judgment day that functions symbolically in the story as Tanner's actual sin of dishonesty to self leading to accepted banishment. By contrast Tanner's original sin, the condition of sinfulness that precedes the individual's actual fall, was his patronizing attitude toward blacks arising from his putative victory, thirty years earlier, over Coleman Parrum. After he had impressed Coleman with his "whittling," a nervous coverup for a more genuine reaction of fear, Tanner rashly concluded: "The secret to handling a nigger was to show him his brains didn't have a chance against yours; then he would jump on your back and know he had a good thing there for life."

This crucial episode, so structurally central to the story, describes a fleeting revelation of human equality that Tanner lacks the spiritual sensibility to recognize. Coleman tries on the pair of spectacles Tanner has whittled from bark, and as he brings Tanner comically into focus, the latter has "an instant's sensation of seeing before him a negative of himself, as if clownishness and captivity had been their common lot. The vision failed him before he could decipher it." In response to Tanner's "What you see through those glasses?" Coleman affirms the experience of equality from his vantage point, "See a man." Responding to "What kind of a man?" Coleman again shows his shrewdness in refusing to yield any more ground than necessary. "See the man make theseyer glasses," he says. Only when Tanner blurts offensively, "Is he white or black?" must Coleman say "He white!"

Through a series of deft narrative transitions O'Connor moves her story from time present (the "morning" of Tanner's day of final judgment) through the recent past of "the morning before" and "two days" before that (when the crisis of where he would be buried arose) into the past at Corinth the day of his exile (when his daughter and Dr. Foley visited him the same day) and finally into the remote past of his original sin of intolerance, the encounter with Coleman that is the structural Cocytus of the tale. The narrative works itself back again to the present along the concentric circles of its temporal descent into recog-

nition, through the day of exile into the near present of
Tanner's stroke and dream of return and the argument
about the place of his burial, then finally into the time
present of his Judgment Day itself.

On the deepest level of meaning, Tanner's sin, like
everyman's, is the original sin of denial of human
brotherhood. His actual sin on the day of racial judgment
in Corinth stems from his refusal to accept the historical
inevitability of changing times. The crisis that Dr. Foley
represents is between classes as well as races—the social
cataclysm that Faulkner in *Absalom, Absalom!* announces
as the future of the Jim Bonds of the world. The level of
the offense is not fraternal as in Tanner's denial of
Coleman, but social and historical. Tanner will accept exile
in New York, where he knows he does not belong, rather
than work for the part black, part Indian and white Dr.
Foley. "The day is coming," Dr. Foley reminds Tanner,
"when the white folks IS going to be working for the
colored and you mights well to git ahead of the crowd."
Tanner's weak response—"That day ain't coming for
me"—is devastated by the stinging truth of Foley's retort:
"Done come for you. . . . Ain't come for the rest of
them." Inasmuch as Dr. Foley's statement is prophetic of
the story's conclusion, it reveals Tanner's death as the
necessary effect of this day's tragic miscalculation.

The dream is the narrative device that O'Connor uses so
successfully in evoking the tone of ultimate victory.
Tanner, knowing that he cannot trust his daughter, decides
to get himself back home—dead or alive—while the
decision is still his to make. Although he has seriously
misjudged the nature of his illness, his determination has
taken him through remote phases of planning. His sense of
expectation erupts into a dream that is pure wish-
fulfillment; in it he arrives home in Corinth in a pine box,
alive enough to scare his cronies half to death with the cry,
"Judgement Day! Judgement Day! . . . Don't you two
fools know it's Judgement Day!" On Tanner's last day,
with the instructions concerning his destination pinned

inside his coat, he totters into the hallway, lurches toward the stairs and lands "upsidedown in the middle of the flight." The jolt of the fall becomes in his imagination the unrelieved joy of a coffin sliding off the baggage wagon in Corinth. Confusing the black actor with Coleman, he delivers the insult that hastens his death and the pronouncement of history's verdict. "Ain't any coal man, either," the actor mocks. ". . . Ain't no judgement day, old man. Cept this. Maybe this here judgement day for you."

The day of interracial judgment, and the tragic convergence it implies, is also Tanner's Homecoming. His final plea to his estranged neighbor—"Hep me up, Preacher. I'm on my way home!"—captures the pathos of conflict and resolution, of sin and forgiveness, of time and eternity. Liberated forever from the "pigeon-hutch of a building" where he atoned for his sins against self and neighbor, Tanner faces joyously the eternal homecoming of his return to Corinth that he is confident he has won.[44]

Carter Martin's judicious assessment of the "remarkable achievement" of "Judgement Day" includes a passing reference to "material that is otherwise pathetic, ugly, and violent."[45] But the ignorance and intolerance that erupt into the violent moment of racial judgment at the story's end seem so understandably commonplace and regrettably familiar that I find it difficult to see them as either "pathetic" or "ugly." Tanner's bumptious stupidity and the black actor's swollen rage are the sparks of everyday tragedy; they are problems so recognizably American and unmistakably human that to deny them is in a sense to deny ourselves.

Although "Judgement Day" is typical of the more explicit hermeneutical pattern of the later stories, it nevertheless stands with respect to O'Connor's other short fiction and particularly to its embryonic version "The Geranium" as one of her finest and subtlest tales, masterful in narrative structure and compelling in tone and effect. This "unmistakable evocation of joy and spiritual triumph,"[46] in Martin's words, is a truly distinguished

American variation on the archetype of homecoming and perhaps our noblest literary presentation of the significance of resurrection.

4: The Novels

THE SAME HERMENEUTIC PATTERN THAT O'CONNOR USED so successfully in most of her stories—particularly in the collections—is less obviously present, but nonetheless demonstrable, in her two novels. It is almost invariably harder to expose the unifying structure of a novel than of a short story because the novel's greater elasticity of form diffuses its "dramatic center." In a novel the dynamism of movement or development, for example, is usually even more pronounced than the presence of conflict. Whereas the term "dramatic center" may be appropriate for the focused conflict of a short story, it seems more reasonable to think of the "dramatic movement" of a novel. Linguistic patterns support the development of both of O'Connor's novels; word illumines their meaning, even fully, although *The Violent Bear It Away* is more subtly effective than *Wise Blood* as an interpretive parable.

I

Aside from Driskell's and Brittain's elaborate treatment of the archlike structure of *Wise Blood*, Sister Kathleen Feeley is apparently the first to fully utilize the framing statements about home made by Mrs. Wally Bee Hitchcock and Mrs. Flood as a vehicle of meaning for the novel. Feeley writes: "[Mrs. Hitchcock's] first statement to Hazel—'I guess you're going home,' introduces the theme of the novel. Her second comment, 'Well . . . there's no place like home,' establishes her cliché-prone mentality, but it does more: it epitomizes Hazel's spiritual displacement, which the entire story unfolds."[1] Emphasizing the parallel prominence of these "normal" characters in the first and last chapters of the novel, Feeley concludes: "The landlady's final words suggest the fulfillment of Haze's spiritual quest. Gazing at the lifeless body on her bed, Mrs. Flood says, 'Well, Mr. Motes . . . I see you've come home.' "[2]

These opening and closing references to home do indeed point to the story's meaning, not only because of the hermeneutic function of language but also because of their symbolic setting and emphatic position. What Sister Kathleen Feeley did not mention was that in keeping with a persistent tripartite pattern in the novel Mrs. Hitchcock and Mrs. Flood each make three references to home in speaking to Hazel Motes. And if the symbolic repetition of the statements were not enough indication of O'Connor's intentions in the transformation of "The Train" into *Wise Blood's* first chapter, she made her interpretive word quite audible by giving it emphatic status. "The Train," as we have noted, places initial importance on the porter and the berth-coffin that Haze will occupy; Mrs. Hosen's query "Are you going home?" although significant to the story's meaning also, comes later. The novel, however, begins with Haze and Mrs. Hitchcock facing one another; her opening attempt to draw him into conversation, the novel's first abortive dialogue, yields meaning beyond her awareness.

Feeley neglects to mention Mrs. Hitchcock's third attempt at dialogue with Haze: the blunt question, "Are you going home?" For the first time in this triple incantation, Haze responds. On the literal level, his response—"No, I ain't"—is not only true but also inevitable: Eastrod is a ghost town, his mother's house an empty shell. Mentioning that he is "going to Taulkinham," even though he "don't know nobody there," Haze converts the negation of a particular destination—home—into the denial of any real destination: "You might as well go one place as another. . . . That's all I know." This second confession of his is actually an

appropriate response to Mrs. Hitchcock's second plati-
tudinous comment about home, "There's no place like
home." Haze's final observation, completing his delayed
three-part answer to the probing references to home,
relates displacement to the absence of experienced
redemption. "I reckon you think you been redeemed" is
his apparently unsolicited and embarrassing assertion. He is
in effect answering Mrs. Hitchcock's final challenge, her
direct question; we can safely assume that "going home,"
on its most profound level, is a matter of redemption.
Haze's eventual responses to his fellow traveler's utterances
become the threefold pattern of denial underlying the
novel's theme: no home, no place, no redemption.

A parallel pattern appears in the final chapter in Mrs.
Flood's three references to home. She has adjusted
sufficiently to Haze's bizarre conduct to permit consideration of the possibility of marriage to her sick tenant. Her
proposal is motivated by combined maternal and economic
needs (Haze receives a disability pension from the govern-
ment) as well as by sloth. "I been thinking," she says,
"how we could arrange it so you would have a home and
somebody to take care of you and I wouldn't have to
climb these stairs. . . ." Apparently fearing further entrapment in decaying relationships, Haze makes no verbal
response but continues dressing, despite the foul weather
and his advanced illness. That Haze plans departure if not
flight is evident from the conclusion of Mrs. Flood's
monologue: ". . . what you dressing for today, Mr. Motes?
You don't want to go out in this weather." Haze is clearly
in extremis; there is no home for him of the sort Mrs.
Flood offers. Undaunted, the landlady pursues her objective: "Nobody ought to be without a place of their own to
be, . . . and I'm willing to give you a home here with me, a
place where you can always stay, Mr. Motes, and never
worry yourself about." Her second invitation provokes
Haze's only spoken reply as his uninterrupted packing
leads her to ask whether he is going to some other city.
"That's not where I'm going," he says. "There's no other

house nor no other city." He may be leaving the house, but he is not going anywhere in a physical sense. Haze no longer assumes that there is no real place to be; he implies that it does not matter where one is provided he redeems the time.

Mrs. Flood's third reference to home, introducing the novel's brief final monologue, is her poignant welcome to her dead tenant. His body is indeed "lifeless" when she addresses him, but Mrs. Flood does not realize immediately that Haze is dead, contrary to Kathleen Feeley's implication.[3] "Well, Mr. Motes," she says behind the locked door of her bedroom, "I see you've come home!" The only meaning she can possibly attach to her exclamation is a literal one, but for the reader who knows that Haze is dead the literal reading alone is hardly sufficient. Even simple irony is less than the context demands, precisely because of the threefold pattern of the novel's interpretive language.

The third reference to home as established in the opening chapter relates to redemption, and indeed the open sockets of Haze's blinded eyes draw the confused Mrs. Flood into the very presence of mystery; those eyes whose depths had first fascinated Mrs. Hitchcock and then Mrs. Flood still communicate. Mrs. Hitchcock had found that "their settings were so deep that they seemed, to her, almost like passages leading somewhere and she leaned halfway across the space that separated the two seats, trying to see into them." That Haze eventually blinds himself in paradoxical expectation of the vision of death is clear from his assuring Mrs. Flood that he believes the dead are blind. "If there's no bottom in your eyes," he says enigmatically, "they hold more." Physical blindness does not prevent genuine vision, it enhances it. The blind Haze gives Mrs. Flood the impression that he is "seeing something. His face had a peculiar pushing look, as if it were going forward after something it could just distinguish in the distance." While he is away from the house, during his last delirious excursion, Mrs. Flood keeps "thinking of his eyes without any bottom in them and of the blindness of death."

In death, Haze's face is "more composed" than it has ever been; doubtlessly we are to conclude that Haze has found what was in the distance. The sockets of his eyes draw Mrs. Flood tantalizingly close to the threshold of revelation; what she sees, however, is only the pinpoint of vanishing opportunity:

> . . . the deep burned eye sockets seemed to lead into the dark tunnel where he had disappeared. She leaned closer and closer to his face, looking deep into them, trying to see how she had been cheated or what had cheated her, but she couldn't see anything. She shut her eyes and saw the pin point of light but so far away that she could not hold it steady in her mind. She felt as if she were blocked at the entrance to something. She sat staring with her eyes shut, into his eyes, and felt as if she had finally got to the beginning of something she couldn't begin, and she saw him moving farther and farther away, farther and farther into the darkness until he was the pin point of light.

The entrance is blocked to her because her vision is limited to temporal coordinates: the only home for her is her boarding-house, the only place is with her ("No other place to be but mine," she had told Haze); the only redemption is the ministry of her care. Haze on the other hand has found his genuine homecoming in death as passage into mystery. The "something" blocked to Mrs. Flood became a possibility for him when he realized that history offers no lasting home, that any place is pregnant with possibility, and that there is indeed no redemption until man understands and accepts the need for it.

The structural prominence of these illuminative references to home is heightened by the symbolic triple repetition. Not only is solemnity achieved through the repetition, it also clearly alludes to the numinous. The Bible is replete with instances where the number three is

related to the sacred. The message that Abraham's barren
wife Sarah will bear a child is brought by three men; Job
has three counselors as he explores God's unfathomable
ways; Jesus is transfigured in the company of Moses and
Elijah, and Peter asks whether three tabernacles should be
erected; Peter denies his master three times before he
realizes the seriousness of his transgression but later makes
a threefold protestation of love. Blessings, invocations, and
apostrophes are quite commonly done in three's. The most
significant scriptural instance of the number from a
Christian viewpoint, however, is Jesus' resurrection from
the dead on the third day; in Christian theology, it is the
number associated with the most sacred of all mysteries,
the persons of the Trinity. Even outside the Judaeo-
Christian world, three is a number of dignity. Pythagoras
called it "the number of completion, expressive of a
beginning, a middle, and an end."[4] It is scarcely by
chance, then, that O'Connor's novel is framed by a solemn
threefold sequence and permeated with three's of varying
importance. The most obvious use of three's appears in
material related to Enoch Emery, particularly in chapters 5
and 8, but the repetition there has a superstitious, even
magical effect.[5] Where the patterns are more subtle as in
the framing sequences and in Haze's relationships, the
repetition creates an aura of mystery.

There are three additional early references to home, one
in each of the three chapters following the first, that keep
the novel's interpretive language in plain view. Each is a
parody of the ultimate affirmation that the novel makes
about home. When Haze tells Mrs. Leora Watts, "I come
for the usual business," the woman advertised as having
"the friendliest bed in town!" says simply, "Make yourself
at home," an invitation that Haze is innately indisposed to
accept. The peeler salesman, trying to con Haze into a
purchase, asks, "Whyn't you take one of these home to yer
wife?" and, discovering that Haze has neither wife nor
mother, jests with the crowd at his expense, "Well
pshaw, . . . he needs one theseyer just to keep him com-

pany." In the third instance, the machine that assumes the function of both home and company for Haze is actually "a high rat-colored machine with large thin wheels and bulging headlights." Haze explains to the used car dealer, "I wanted this car mostly to be a house for me. . . . I ain't got any place to be." The parody of home is reduced to an absurdity when a driver whose car Haze is blocking walks up and asks impatiently, "Will you get your goddam outhouse off the middle of the road?"

Aside from the emphatic position given the introductory discussion of home, the most important addition to the pre-*Wise Blood* stories as revised for the novel is also in chapter 1, where O'Connor expands Haze's dream sequence from "The Train" to provide the necessary motivation for his religious odyssey. The kernel of the novel's developing word is embedded in the rich metaphoric soil of this flashback. The account of Haze's background as well as the substance of his preaching plumb depths of meaning that the *Wise Blood* stories even as a cycle never approach. Haze is to an extent the victim of his grandfather's ridicule. Although a rural evangelist whose power like every preacher's was "in his neck and tongue and arm," Haze's grandfather would use the boy disdainfully as an example of Jesus' mercy for the sake of the "stone souls" gathered around his car—and as a compensation for his own insecurity. (The grandfather's disdain stemmed from his awareness that "his own face was repeated almost exactly in the child's and seemed to mock him.") "Even for that boy there, for that mean sinful unthinking boy standing there with his dirty hands clenching and unclenching at his sides," he would say of Haze, "Jesus would die ten million deaths before He would let him lose his soul."

But Haze has his own inner conviction that makes him receptive to this fundamentalist word: "The boy didn't need to hear it. There was already a deep black wordless conviction in him that the way to avoid Jesus was to avoid sin. . . . Later he saw Jesus move from tree to tree in the

back of his mind, a wild ragged figure motioning him to
turn around and come off into the dark where he was not
sure of his footing, where he might be walking on the
water and not know it and then suddenly know it and
drown." In one of O'Connor's most apposite metaphors
the experience of mystery is imagined as a summons to
walk into the uncertain dark out of the plastic clarity of
the tried and true. Haze's reaction to the summons is
man's characteristic fear of the unknown: "Where he
wanted to stay was in Eastrod with his own two eyes open,
and his hands always handling the familiar thing, his feet
on the known track, and his tongue not too loose."
"Going home" is accepting the summons into mystery as
reality's invitation to man to acknowledge the stony
burden of the spirit which is the inertia of our mortal flesh
and to embrace the darkness of radical dependence—"to
turn around and come off into the dark." The narrative
chronicles the process of Haze's reluctant admission of the
burden of his flesh (the sin that "came before") and of his
ultimate symbolic act of reverence for mystery in his ritual
self-blinding.

In a manner typical of assertive man, Haze's "coming
off" is not a simple "turning around." Before acknowledging man's heritage of sin, he abandons the assurance of
"the familiar thing" to embrace the folly of "nothing
instead." In the world of O'Connor's work "the familiar
thing" is of course neutral, the Gospel salt that has no
flavor. Leaving neutral ground Haze opts for the emptiness
of nothing over the fullness of mystery. Rather than
believe that going to a brothel with his army friends would
be sinful ("the way to avoid Jesus was to avoid sin"), he
finds in his seeming abandonment by the army an excuse
to believe with them that "he didn't have any soul":

> He took a long time to believe them because he wanted
> to believe them. All he wanted was to believe them and
> get rid of [his soul] once and for all, and he saw the
> opportunity here to get rid of it without corruption, to
> be converted to nothing instead of to evil. The army

sent him halfway around the world and forgot him. He was wounded and they remembered him long enough to take the shrapnel out of his chest—they said they took it out but they never showed it to him and he felt it still in there, rusted, and poisoning him—and then they sent him to another desert and forgot him again. He had all the time he could want to study his soul in and assure himself that it was not there. When he was thoroughly convinced, he saw that this was something that he had always known. The misery he had was a longing for home; it had nothing to do with Jesus.

The home that he wants to return to is actually the neutrality of the past—the only "nothing" that the novel acknowledges. The past as home is the death of an abandoned town and the decay of naked flesh.

There is literally no place that Haze can return to, but he can legitimately "turn around" to an acceptance of his own poverty; this kind of "conversion" is of course a way to "come off into the dark," not a "going back." It is in the context of Haze's conversion that the novel's dualism emerges—not the radical dualism of good and evil that Stanley Edgar Hyman finds,[6] but rather a reasonable structural variation on the Pauline discrimination between flesh and spirit or at least an elaboration of the Greek dichotomy of body and soul. These are of the same fundamental order, not of opposing orders as a radical dualism of sources would imply; in *Wise Blood*, both flesh and spirit revolt against the summons to humility.

The apocalyptic warning that Haze sees painted on a boulder in white letters, the first time he takes the road in his Essex, suggests that it is the whole man, whoring flesh and blasphemous spirit, that resists the invitation to accept life's mystery: "WOE TO THE BLASPHEMER AND WHOREMONGER! WILL HELL SWALLOW YOU UP?" Haze's response to the sign is a first indication of his notional assent to the limitation of the human condition that he will eventually convert into real assent. "There's no person a whoremonger, who wasn't something worse first. . . . That's not the sin, nor blasphemy. The sin came before them." Haze's simple language reflects of course the theological sophistication of his creator; as in his earlier encounter with the false preacher Asa Hawks, he is unwilling to admit sin as pure malice: there is an inclination in man toward evil that precedes any personal decision (original sin in traditional Christian terminology). In keeping with the novel's consistent division of actual sins into those of flesh and spirit, Hawks rejects Haze's "I'm as clean as you are" and guesses his sins, "Fornication and blasphemy and what else?" "They ain't nothing but words," Haze declares, with greater initial assurance than his conditional afterthought, "If I was in sin I was in it before I ever committed any." Once again at the conclusion of this episode, when the narrative shifts abruptly to time past as it had in "The Peeler," reference is appropriately made to the *sin* that precedes *sins*. When his preadolescent curiosity was aroused by the nude woman in the coffin, Haze quickly "forgot the guilt of the tent for the nameless unplaced guilt that was in him." The "stones and small rocks" that he placed in his shoes for a brief period, thinking with the simplicity of a child, "That ought to satisfy Him," become later on the permanent penitential companions of his last days when he walks on them "to pay." Then he possesses a knowledge he cannot communicate to Mrs. Flood and an adult conviction that does not expect a sign.

The sequence of Haze's exposure to the effects of man's unfinished nature remains intact from the first three *Wise Blood* stories, even though the tone of Haze's experience of death as the inaccessibility of the past (his Eastrod home) has been greatly altered through the introduction of the novel's explicit religious dimension. Mortality (berth-coffin) and concupiscence of the flesh (the peeler), Haze discovers in the heart of the park, are the result of man's natural poverty, his corporeal link with the animal kingdom. In these three episodes the novel, like the stories, dramatizes the essential features of that "nameless unplaced guilt," the sin that we are *in* before we commit any.

In view of the novel's recurring patterns of three's, it is hardly surprising that there would be three exemplars of sins of the flesh and three of sins of the spirit. The woman in the carnival side show, Leora Watts, and Sabbath Lily Hawks all represent fornication; and the spiritual con men Asa Hawks, Hoover Shoats, and Solace Layfield all blaspheme for the sake of money. As for Haze's actual sins of fornication and blasphemy, he will not admit them until he experiences a triple exposure to their dual lie. From the curiosity of the carnival tent, through the clumsy experimentation of Leora Watts's darkened room, to the more relaxed "romance" with Sabbath Lily, Haze discovers the absolute destitution of sexual license. The threefold process traces a pattern from innate inclination to willing consent. Sabbath Lily confesses to Haze that she thinks "he's just pure filthy right down to the guts, like [her]," but "the only difference is [she likes] being that way and he don't." Before climbing into bed with the "king of the beasts," she asks him, "Don't you want to learn how to like it?" and he answers unequivocally, "Yeah, . . . I want to." The pathetic product of their union is the mummy Enoch steals to be Haze's "new jesus"; Sabbath cradles it like an infant in whom "there was something . . . of everyone she had ever known, as if they had all been rolled into one person and killed and shrunk and dried." In the first of a series of three climactic acts of violence, each of which image of recognition, "daddy" destroys the Even the nihil built on his lust.

The system that Haze preaches and wants to believe is built on a blasphemy of three's. He offers curious bystanders a "Church Without Christ . . . where the blind don't see and the lame don't walk and what's dead stays that way." From the three marks of his church, he proceeds to explain its triple theological foundation. "I'm going to preach there was no Fall," he says, "because there was nothing to fall from and no Redemption because there was no Fall and no Judgment because there wasn't the first two. Nothing matters but that Jesus was a liar." As empirical proof that there is no fall, no redemption, and no judgment, he asks his listeners to point to the place in time and body where Jesus has redeemed them: "In yourself right now is all the place you got. If there was any Fall, look there, if there was any Redemption, look there, and if you expect any Judgment, look there, because they all three will have to be in your time and your body and where in your time and your body can they be?" Haze's ultimate expression of nihilism—that there is "no truth" behind each individual's truth—extends to the absence of any saving place, past, present, or future, outside of the unredeemed self. "No truth behind all truths is what I and this church preach!" he exclaims. "Where you come from is gone, where you thought you were going to never was there, and where you are is no good unless you can get away from it. Where is there a place for you to be? No place."

The reality of his lie is revealed to him gradually as he uncovers the fraud of his three competitors. Haze has to wait until he strikes a match in the dark and looks into Asa Hawks's eyes to discover that the latter's blindness is a fake and his promise to blind himself to justify his belief in Jesus a blasphemy. When the accomplished con artist Onnie Jay Holy sees Haze's preaching as an opportunity to fleece the people and jumps on the Essex offering three reasons why people should trust Haze's church—"it's nothing foreign," "it's based on the Bible," and "[it's] up-to-date"—Haze responds vehemently, "This man is a liar. . . . I never saw him before tonight." Rejected, Onnie Jay Holy (really Hoover Shoats, a name appropriate to his demonic personality), promises "to run [Haze] out of business": he creates Haze's spiritual alter ego out of the "hired Prophet" Solace Layfield—"a man in a glare-blue suit and white hat" with "a loud consumptive cough." The second act of violence like the first is perpetrated by Haze; as he knocks Solace down with the Essex and runs over

him, he destroys the image of his own pretentious lie.
"You ain't true. . . . You believe in Jesus," Haze observes,
going on to insist, "Two things I can't stand . . . a man that
ain't true and one that mocks what is." Chagrined and
furious, Haze is forced to listen to the dying man's
confession. Solace's lie by comparison with Haze's had
been a simple adjustment to financial necessity.

The following morning as Haze hastens "to another
city," cursing and blaspheming and equivalently "believing
in something to blaspheme," a hostile patrolman pushes
the Essex over an embankment because Haze is driving
without a license: "The car landed on its top, with the
three wheels that stayed on, spinning" (my emphasis). This
third gratuitous act of violence, depriving Haze of his last
claim to independence—"Nobody with a good car needs to
be justified," he bragged—stuns him into realizing that
"there [is] not another city," that in preaching *nothing* he
was actually going *nowhere.*[7] He is prepared at last to
"turn around and come off into the dark"; his ritual
blinding is a preference for the darkness of mystery over
the nihilism of blasphemous self-sufficiency; his penitential
stones and barbed wire an acceptance of his unfinished
nature against the absurd denial of human limitation.[8]
Enoch Emery's regression to animality is an ironic inversion of Haze's spiritual ascent. To boast of "wise blood" is,
in the final analysis, the ultimate human folly.[9] There is
no home or wisdom apart from the conceded indigence of
the flesh and the paradoxical vision of blindness.

II

O'Connor's most sustained and compelling use of
interpretive language is undoubtedly found in her second
novel, *The Violent Bear It Away.* The central dramatic
metaphor, linking the three principal characters of the
novel—Mason, Rayber, and Tarwater—is taken appropriately from the New Testament parable of the Sower. It is

Mason who has sown the seed of God's word in both his nephew and his grandnephew. Although Mason's opportunity to instruct Rayber had been short-lived, he had had more freedom in educating Tarwater to the life of prophecy, a mission considerably more complex and enduring than the simple insistence on Christian burial that lies at the heart of the dramatic conflict in "You Can't Be Any Poorer Than Dead." In the novel, "the old man, who said he was a prophet, had raised the boy to expect the Lord's call himself." And because Mason is a prophet of the New Covenant, the word that he plants in Tarwater's heart is a radical hunger for the bread of life. In Rayber the effect of the seed is a chronic impulse to love that is ironically stimulated by the presence of his idiot child.

When Mason had baptized the infant Tarwater in Rayber's house, the nephew had adverted to his own misfortune in having been seduced by the old man when he was seven years old rather than only seven days like Tarwater. Nevertheless, Rayber had insisted, "I've straightened the tangle you made. Straightened it by pure will power. I've made myself straight." Narrating the encounter later for Tarwater's benefit, Mason adds: "You see, . . . he admitted himself the seed was still in him." The seed remains in Rayber's blood as the "curse" of love, for when he least expected it he would experience a love for Bishop "so outrageous that he would be left shocked and depressed for days"; the sudden urge to love his idiot child "was only a touch of the curse that lay in his blood. . . . He always felt with it a rush of longing to have the old man's eyes . . . turned on him once again. The longing was like an undertow in his blood dragging him backwards to what he knew to be madness. . . . The affliction was in the family. It lay hidden in the line of blood that touched them, flowing from some ancient source, some desert prophet or polesitter, until, its power unabated, it appeared in the old man and him and, he surmised, in the boy."

Driving to Powderhead with Bishop from the Cherokee

Lodge, Rayber is unable to suppress "unpleasant thoughts" about "his terrifying love" focused in the child: "He felt a sinister pull on his consciousness, the familiar undertow of expectation, as if he were still a child waiting on Christ." The seed planted in his youthful blood is the "undertow of expectation" that would draw him back through the years to the springtime of insemination. The effect of the seed sown in Rayber directly by Mason—the inexplicable desire to love—is of course the latter-day result of a far earlier planting.

That Mason was aware of the irrevocable power of the word he had sown is clear from Rayber's recollection of the day when his father had "rescued" him from the old man. Rayber had told Mason:

> "He's going to take me back with him."
> "Back with him where?" his uncle growled. "He ain't got any place to take you back to."
> "He can't take me back with him?"
> "Not where you were before."
> "He can't take me back to town?"
> "I never said nothing about town," his uncle said.

Commenting years later on the effect of his brief period of control over Rayber's education, Mason reminds Tarwater that "the first place [Rayber] came" after the accident in which his father, mother, and sister were killed was "straight out" to Powderhead:

> ". . . The truth was even if they told him not to believe what I had taught him, he couldn't forget it. He never could forget that there was a chance that that simpleton was not his only father. I planted the seed in him and it was there for good. Whether anybody liked it or not."
> "It fell amongst cockles," Tarwater said. . . .
> "It fell in deep," the old man said, "or else after that crash he wouldn't have come out here hunting me."

There is a wisdom in Tarwater's estimate of Rayber's capacity to receive the word that clearly exceeds his momentary desire to irritate the old man. During a final

confrontation between Rayber and Tarwater, the schoolteacher, "rigidly keeping the exasperation out of his
voice," reminds the boy, "The old man still has you in his
grip." It is Tarwater then who volunteers the parabolic
metaphor:

> "It's you the seed fell in," he said. "It ain't a thing you
> can do about it. It fell on bad ground but it fell in deep.
> With me," he said proudly, "it fell on rock and the wind
> carried it away."
>   The schoolteacher grasped the table as if he were
> going to push it forward into the boy's chest. "Goddam
> you!" he said in a breathless harsh voice. "It fell in us
> both alike. The difference is that I know it's in me and I
> keep it under control. I weed it out but you're too blind
> to know it's in you."

Persisting in his perverse determination to imagine the
word yielding weeds, Rayber later insists that all Tarwater
need do is confront faith with intelligence. "The other
way," he inveighs, "is simply to face it and fight it, to cut
down the weed every time you see it appear. Do I have to
tell you this? An intelligent boy like you?"
    This discussion precedes Tarwater's experience of ulti-
mate personal evil when he is raped by the homosexual; he
is still consciously deluding himself about the effect of the
word in him. He is thus finally more accurate in his
estimate of the word's effect on Rayber when talking to
Mason than he is in answering Rayber himself; proximity
to the source of irritation consistently distorts Tarwater's
perspective. Rayber is certainly bad ground, but the word
had fallen "in deep" only as a sterile, lasting goad, hardly
as a fertile germ. In one of O'Connor's most telling
variations on the image of the seed, the roots of Rayber's
peace are described as slender. Tarwater's perversity
arouses the dormant fury in Rayber, stored up over the
years in response to Mason's early sowing: "[Rayber's]
fury seemed to be stirring from buried depths that had lain

quiet for years and to be working upward, closer and closer, toward the slender roots of his peace."

The parable of the sower finds even more pointed affirmation in significant descriptive passages related to Tarwater. During a typically repetitious lesson in the history of family prophecy, when Mason would recount how he had prophesied on his sister's doorstep (the day she had him committed to the asylum), Tarwater would take up a shotgun and sight along it, pretending not to be listening. Mason told how he had shouted at his sister hidden within the house: "Ignore the Lord Jesus as long as you can! Spit out the bread of life and sicken on honey. . . . The Lord is preparing a prophet with fire in his hand and eye and the prophet is moving toward the city with his warning." On such an occasion, Tarwater "would lift his face from the gun for a moment with a look of uneasy alertness, as if while he had been inattentive, the old man's words had been dropping one by one into him and now, silent, hidden in his bloodstream, were moving secretly toward some goal of their own."

Until the climactic moment in the novel when Tarwater deliberately turns his face "toward the dark city, where the children of God lay sleeping," his lack of experience of the world's capacity to inflict evil and his adolescent desire to have his own way conspired within him to repress the growth of the seed that in him had indeed fallen "in deep." Tarwater, intimately aware of the horror of evil through his exploitation by the homosexual stranger, hears the renewed command of his great-uncle; "GO WARN THE CHILDREN OF GOD OF THE TERRIBLE SPEED OF MERCY. The words," we are told, "were as silent as seeds *opening* one at a time in his blood" (my emphasis). Mason had sown that word carefully in the soil of Tarwater's spirit in studied vindication of his prophetic warning to Rayber: "THE PROPHET I RAISE UP OUT OF THIS BOY WILL BURN YOUR EYES CLEAN."

The seed that Tarwater ultimately allows to sprout in his free acceptance of the prophetic call had from his

earliest consciousness of it aroused in him, as the kernel of
Mason's teaching, a hunger for the "bread of life": "The
boy sensed that this was the heart of his great-uncle's
madness, this hunger, and what he was secretly afraid of
was that it might be passed down, might be hidden in the
blood and might strike some day in him and then he would
be torn by hunger like the old man, the bottom split out
of his stomach so that nothing would heal or fill it but the
bread of life."

Tarwater, throughout his period of formation, found
the Jesus whom Mason preached as the bread of life
altogether "unremarkable" as a subject of prophecy (and
an object of hunger); his deep preference was for a call
that would manifest itself in the cosmic display of a still
sun or at least a burning bush—IF indeed he must be called
at all. Tarwater's penchant for the images of the Old
Testament over the New is at the heart of his aversion to
prophecy. Is Jesus—the bread of life!—all that comes of
that great history of fire, sun, and beasts?

> In the darkest, most private part of his soul, hanging
> upsidedown like a sleeping bat, was the certain, undeni-
> able knowledge that he was not hungry for the bread of
> life. Had the bush flamed for Moses, the sun stood still
> for Joshua, the lions turned aside before Daniel only to
> prophesy the bread of life? Jesus? He felt a terrible
> disappointment in that conclusion, a dread that it was
> true. The old man said that as soon as he died, he would
> hasten to the banks of the Lake of Galilee to eat the
> loaves and fishes that the Lord had multiplied.

Despite the moment of "certain, undeniable knowledge,"
there is a persistent and perplexing dread that Mason's
account of salvation history is true. If something as
ordinary as hunger—"this threatened intimacy of creation"—can determine one's call then discipline is necessary, Tarwater concludes, to avoid seduction by such a
commonplace sign.

> He tried when possible to pass over these thoughts, to
> keep his vision located on an even level, to see no more

than what was in front of his face and to let his eyes stop at the surface of that. It was as if he were afraid that if he let his eye rest for an instant longer than was needed to place something—a spade, a hoe, the mule's hind quarters before his plow, the red furrow under him—that the thing would suddenly stand before him, strange and terrifying, demanding that he name it and name it justly and be judged for the name he gave it. He did all he could to avoid this threatened intimacy of creation. When the Lord's call came, he wished it to be a voice from out of a clear and empty sky, the trumpet of the Lord God Almighty, untouched by any fleshy hand or breath. He expected to see wheels of fire in the eyes of unearthly beasts.

Predictably, Tarwater preferred the fierce cast to Mason's eyes after his periodic bouts with the Lord over his handling of Rayber's training; Mason had recurring doubts that "he might have helped the nephew on to his new course himself" rather than averted it.

At such times he would wander into the woods and leave Tarwater alone in the clearing, occasionally for days, while he thrashed out his peace with the Lord, and when he returned, bedraggled and hungry, he would look the way the boy thought a prophet ought to look. He would look as if he had been wrestling a wildcat, as if his head were still full of the visions he had seen in its eyes, wheels of light and strange beasts with giant wings of fire and four heads turned to the four points of the universe. These were the times that Tarwater knew that when he was called, he would say, "Here I am, Lord, ready!" At other times when there was no fire in his uncle's eye and he spoke only of the sweat and stink of the cross, of being born again to die, and of spending eternity eating the bread of life, the boy would let his mind wander off to other subjects.

And whenever his great-uncle would remind him that even though "the servants of the Lord Jesus could expect the worse" their reward in the end was "the bread of life," "the boy would have a hideous vision of himself sitting forever with his great-uncle on a green bank, full and sick, staring at a broken fish and a multiplied loaf."

Though hunger is the only sign that Tarwater is ever given, he persists, even through his eleventh-hour acceptance of the call, in comparing the given with the more desirable "unmistakable" signs awarded to the prophets of the Old Testament. When he knocked at Rayber's door for the first time, "his whole body felt hollow as if he had been lifted like Habakkuk by the hair of his head, borne swiftly through the night and set down in the place of his mission." Seeing Bishop produced an immediate revelation that was "silent, implacable, direct as a bullet. He did not look into the eyes of any fiery beast or see a burning bush. . . . He knew that he was called to be a prophet and that the ways of his prophecy would not be remarkable. His black pupils, glassy and still, reflected depth on depth his own stricken image of himself, trudging into the distance in the bleeding stinking mad shadow of Jesus, until at last he received his reward, a broken fish, a multiplied loaf." His seductive friend, the stranger within, however,

was adamant that he refuse to entertain hunger as a sign. He pointed out that the prophets had been fed. Elijah had lain down under a juniper tree to die and had gone to sleep and an angel of the Lord had come and waked him and fed him a hearth-cake, had done it moreover twice and Elijah had risen and gone about his business, lasting on the two hearth-cakes forty days and nights. Prophets did not languish in hunger but were fed from the Lord's bounty and the signs given them were unmistakable. His friend suggested he demand an unmistakable sign, not a pang of hunger or a reflection of himself in a store window, but an unmistakable sign, clear and suitable—water bursting forth from a rock, for instance, fire sweeping down at his command and destroying some site he would point to. . . .

Even in the end when he purifies himself in ritual rejection of his inner voice, he still wants to believe that "the red-gold tree of fire" that he ignites is "the fire that had encircled Daniel, that had raised Elijah from the earth, that had spoken to Moses and would in the instant speak to him."

It is certainly intended irony that O'Connor describes Mason in terms of the object of the hunger he preaches and Bishop, the living reminder of his prophetic legacy, as an avatar of the old man. Since Mason's more immediate concern in training Tarwater was to leave a Christian to bury him properly, his lessons in personal history frequently turned to the moment of death; with foresight appropriate to his ultimate concern, Mason had built his own coffin "and when he had finished it, he had scratched on the lid, MASON TARWATER, WITH GOD, and had climbed into it where it stood on the back porch, and had lain there some time, nothing showing but his stomach which rose over the top like over-leavened bread." In response to the boy's reminder that Rayber would burn his body if given the chance, Mason retorted, "I been leavened by the yeast he don't believe in, . . . and I won't be burned!" At the moment of his death, the old man's "silver protruding eyes . . . looked like two fish straining to get out of a net of red threads." And Bishop, whose name appropriately means "overseer," who "had pale silver eyes like the old man's except that they were clear and empty," "looked like the old man grown backwards to the lowest form of innocence."

For Rayber and Tarwater, Bishop represents the enduring focal point of the "threatened intimacy of creation" that Mason's word had warned them to expect. Both exercise relentless discipline on his account. Tarwater, as we have seen, never lets "his eye rest for an instant longer than [is] needed to place something." He refrains especially from looking at Bishop, and Rayber notes it: "I nurse an idiot that you're afraid to look at. . . . Look him in the eye." And because Rayber's urge to "love without reason . . . only began with Bishop," he tried to keep his "affliction" under control "by what amounted to a rigid ascetic discipline. He did not look at *anything* too long, he denied his senses unnecessary satisfactions" (my emphasis). He felt that "he could control his terrifying love as long as it had its focus in Bishop" because "his normal way of looking on Bishop was an *x* signifying the general hideousness of fate. He did not believe that he himself was formed in the image and likeness of God but that Bishop was he had no doubt." Whatever stability he had "depended on the little boy's presence," but "if anything happened to the child, he would have to face it in itself. Then the whole world would become his idiot child. He had thought what he would have to do if anything happened to Bishop. He would have with one supreme effort to resist the recognition; with every nerve and muscle and thought, he would have to resist feeling anything at all, thinking anything at all. He would have to anesthetize his life." Bishop is both the source and limit of Rayber's punishing experience; the love that arises only in Bishop's presence can be contained only within his blasphemous thoughts about the image the child was created in.

Typical of the Gospel parables, it is in response to a simple everyday need of Bishop's that Rayber receives his final invitation to love and that Tarwater is opened definitively, though subconsciously, to the reality of mission. On the way to the museum in the park where Rayber is intending "to stretch [Tarwater's] mind by introducing him to his ancestor, the fish," Bishop's shoelaces come untied and Rayber takes the child into his lap to tie them: "Without warning his hated love gripped him and held him in a vise. He should have known better than to let the child onto his lap." The gesture of humility is the handmaiden of love; in John's account of the last supper, Jesus instructs the apostles to love one another—by washing their feet. A more precise biblical parallel that suggests humility's ancillary role comes from the opening chapter of John's Gospel (1:27), where John the Baptist, precursor of Jesus who *is* love, announces his unworthiness "to undo his shoes." The seed that was sown on apparently worthy soil yields only transitory sprouts of love that are easily choked by the cockles of Rayber's disbelief, his positivistic reluctance to admit the possibility of mystery.

Whereas it is Rayber's instinctual response to Bishop's need that leads to his last unwanted motion of love, Tarwater's act of service follows an apparent submission to creation's threatened intimacy. His intentions are devious though. We observe the change through the fierce gaze of the woman attendant at the Cherokee Lodge, who senses that Tarwater has "profaned the holy" in withdrawing from Bishop's friendly touch: "He looked back at the afflicted child and the woman was startled by the expression on his face. He seemed to see the little boy and nothing else, no air around him, no room, no nothing, as if his gaze had slipped and fallen into the center of the child's eyes and was still falling down and down and down." The relaxation of his normal vigilance over his eyes and his ensuing unexpected kindness in tying the child's shoes presage not only the beginning of his ability to look directly at Bishop—a change that Rayber notices—but also his conscious determination to "do NO" as well as "say NO'" by drowning the child. The roots of the seed in him are so deep that even premeditated violence cannot extirpate them. The baptism-drowning is, as I have tried to demonstrate elsewhere, the compulsive effect of the seed's deep impregnation of Tarwater; by no means a free act on his part, and therefore certainly no signal of his personal acceptance of the prophet's role, the baptism-drowning is an abiding reminder to Tarwater that grace can seize even one's demented efforts to deny it.[10]

Tying Bishop's shoes heralds the end for Rayber; for Tarwater it is a remote beginning. Rayber feared that in the absence of Bishop he would have "to anesthetize his life" rather than let "the whole world . . . become his idiot child." Alone in his room at the Cherokee Lodge he imagines himself awaiting a cataclysm that will turn "all the world . . . into a burnt spot between two chimneys." An instant before he hears the "unmistakable bellow" of his drowning son, Rayber grabs at his hearing aid "as if he were clawing his heart." "The machine," we are told, "made the sounds seem to come from inside him as if something in him were tearing itself free." Rayber's last link with love is of course being wrenched from him, body and soul; the metal box that he grabs as if clawing his heart is with its "dull mechanical beat" all the heart that he has left. Instead of a world consumed by fire, Rayber alone is affected: he experiences the simple annihilation of human emotions. He feels nothing, not even pain; and worse still he realizes that there will be no pain at all.

As perplexing for Tarwater perhaps as the word that Mason had sown in his soul is the effect of the words of baptism that he compulsively pronounces in his very attempt at definitive rejection of a call. Although insisting that what he did is more important than what he said—"the words just come out of themselves but it don't mean nothing"—Tarwater instinctively knows that his enduring hunger is more than an emptiness in his stomach. Thus when he is violated by the homosexual stranger and experiences personally for the first time the evil that prophets are born to rail against, it is *his* eyes that are burned clean, an ironic fulfillment of Mason's prophecy to Rayber, but similar to Mason's own unexpected early purification by the Lord. "His eyes looked small and seedlike as if while he was asleep, they had been lifted out, scorched, and dropped back into his head. His expression seemed to contract until it reached some point beyond rage or pain. Then a loud dry cry tore out of him and his mouth fell back into place." Purifying the places where his body was raped by the homosexual and his mind violated for the last time by the stranger's voice is symbolic not only of his own need to be wholly cleansed but also of his acceptance of a prophetic mission to burn the world clean.

Notes

Introduction

1. Robert Drake, *Flannery O'Connor: A Critical Essay* (Grand Rapids, Mich.: William B. Eerdmans, 1966), p. 14.

2. T.S. Eliot's final resolution of the tension between literature and religion, it should be noted, actually skirted the problem of interpretation and made theology's place in the process of criticism basically a question of evaluation. One must answer the question "Is this literature?" solely on literary grounds, Eliot claimed, but one could never consider literature great without appeal to theological norms. (See chapter 1, n. 1.)

3. E.D. Hirsch, Jr., *Validity in Interpretation* (New Haven: Yale University Press, 1967), p. xi.

4. René Wellek and Austin Warren, *Theory of Literature*, 3rd ed. (New York: Harcourt, Brace & World, 1956), p. 156.

5. Allen D. Lackey, "Flannery O'Connor and Her Critics: A Survey and Evaluation of the Critical Response to the Fiction of Flannery O'Connor" (Ph.D. diss., University of Tennessee, 1972), p. 229.

6. Dorothy Walters, *Flannery O'Connor*, Twayne's United States Authors Series (New York: Twayne Publishers, 1973); Martha Stephens, *The Question of Flannery O'Connor* (Baton Rouge: Louisiana State University Press, 1973), p. 145.

7. Stephens, p. 9.

8. Five of the stories from the collections—"The River," "A Circle in the Fire," "A Late Encounter with the Enemy," "The Enduring Chill," and, surprisingly enough, "Revelation"—have not received individual treatment in the journals, and none of the stories which were uncollected (prior to Giroux's *The Complete Stories*). "A Circle in the Fire" and "Revelation" have, however, received considerable attention in the critical books.

9. Miles Orvell, *Invisible Parade: The Fiction of Flannery O'Connor* (Philadelphia: Temple University Press, 1972), p. 10.

10. Robert Drake, " "The Bleeding Stinking Mad Shadow of Jesus' in the Fiction of Flannery O'Connor," *Comparative Literature Studies* 3 (1966), 188. The label "Gratuitous Grotesque" comes from William Esty, "In America, Intellectual Bomb Shelters," *Commonweal* 67 (March 7, 1958), 586–88; the ensuing dialogue, including discussions of the nature of Southern fiction, of Southern Gothic and the grotesque, has achieved the consensus regarding O'Connor's use of the grotesque. See Robert Detweiler, "The Curse of Christ in Flannery O'Connor's Fiction," *Comparative Literature Studies* 3 (1966), 235–45; Bob Dowell, "The Moment of Grace in the Fiction of Flannery O'Connor," *College English* 27 (December 1965), 235–39; James F. Farnham, "The Grotesque in Flannery O'Connor," *America* 105 (May 13, 1961), 277, 280–81; Jane Hart, "Strange Earth, The Stories of Flannery O'Connor," *Georgia Review* 12 (Summer 1958), 215–22; George Lensing, "De Chardin's Ideas in Flannery O'Connor," *Renascence* 18 (Summer 1966), 171–75; Leonard F. X. Mayhew, "Flannery O'Connor, 1925–64," *Commonweal* 80 (August 21, 1964), 562–63; Robert M. McCown, S.J., "Flannery O'Connor and the Reality of Sin," *Catholic World* 188 (January 1959), 285–91; Marion Montgomery, "The Sense of Violation: Notes Toward a Definition of 'Southern' Fiction," *Georgia Review* 19 (Fall 1965), 278–87; James G. Murray, "Southland *a la Russe*," *The Critic* 21 (June–July 1963), 26–28; Thelma J. Shinn, "Flannery O'Connor and the Violence of Grace," *Contemporary Literature* 9 (Winter 1968), 58–73; Ollye Tine Snow, "The Functional Gothic of Flannery O'Connor," *Southwest Review* 50 (Summer 1965), 286–99; Walter Sullivan, "The Achievement of Flannery O'Connor," *Southern Humanities Review* 2 (Summer 1968), 303–9; Henry Taylor, "The Halt Shall be Gathered Together: Physical Deformity in the Fiction of Flannery O'Connor," *Western Humanities Review* 22 (Autumn 1968), 325–38; and especially Gilbert H. Muller, *Nightmares and Visions: Flannery O'Connor and the Catholic Grotesque* (Athens: University of Georgia Press, 1972).

11. Orvell, *Invisible Parade*, p. 13; Drake, " "The Bleeding Stinking Mad Shadow of Jesus' in the Fiction of Flannery O'Connor," p. 193; Sister Kathleen Feeley, S.S.N.D., *Flannery O'Connor: Voice of the Peacock* (New Brunswick, N.J.: Rutgers University Press, 1972), p. 93.

12. Preston M. Browning, Jr., *Flannery O'Connor* (Carbondale:

Southern Illinois University Press, 1974). For a detailed discussion of the ontological dimensions of the problem, see his, "Flannery O'Connor and the Demonic," *Modern Fiction Studies* 19 (Spring 1973), 29–41. The essay by John Hawkes that triggered the debate was "Flannery O'Connor's Devil," *Sewanee Review* 70 (Summer 1962), 395–407; the significant contributions to the dialogue in order of appearance include Brainard Cheney, "Miss O'Connor Creates Unusual Humor out of Ordinary Sin," *Sewanee Review* 71 (Autumn 1963), 644–52; Thomas Merton, "Flannery O'Connor," *Jubilee* 12 (November 1964), 49, 51–53; John Hawkes, "Scholars, Critics, Writers and the Campus," *Wisconsin Studies in Contemporary Literature* 6 (Summer 1965), 146–47; Thomas F. Walsh, "The Devils of Hawthorne and Flannery O'Connor," *Xavier University Studies* 5 (June 1966), 117–22; William A. Fahey, "Out of the Eater: Flannery O'Connor's Appetite for Truth," *Renascence* 20 (Autumn 1967), 22–29; Marion Montgomery, "Miss Flannery's 'Good Man,'" *Denver Quarterly* 3 (Autumn 1968), 1–19; Ruth M. Vande Kieft, "Judgment in the Fiction of Flannery O'Connor," *Sewanee Review* 76 (Spring 1968), 337–56; and Carter W. Martin, "Flannery O'Connor's Early Fiction," *Southern Humanities Review* 7 (Spring 1973), 210–14.

13. Stanley Edgar Hyman, *Flannery O'Connor*, University of Minnesota Pamphlets on American Writers No. 54 (Minneapolis: University of Minnesota Press, 1966), p. 37.

14. Carter W. Martin, *The True Country: Themes in the Fiction of Flannery O'Connor* (Vanderbilt University Press, 1969), p. 14; Browning, *Flannery O'Connor*, p. 23.

15. Leon V. Driskell and Joan T. Brittain, *The Eternal Crossroads: The Art of Flannery O'Connor* (Lexington: University Press of Kentucky, 1971); David Eggenschwiler, *The Christian Humanism of Flannery O'Connor* (Detroit: Wayne State University Press, 1972).

16. The other three stories, all from the first collection, posing serious critical problems are "A Circle in the Fire," "A Temple of the Holy Ghost," and "The Displaced Person."

17. Josephine Hendin, *The World of Flannery O'Connor* (Bloomington, Ind.: Indiana University Press, 1970), p. 17.

18. Stephens, *The Question of Flannery O'Connor*, p. 47, n. 2. For a fuller analysis of Hendin's work and of the other book-length essays referred to in this Introduction, see my reviews that have appeared in three issues of *The New Orleans Review*: on Hendin, Muller, and Feeley in vol. 3, no. 4 (1973), 385–89; on Eggen-

schwiler, Orvell, Walters, and Driskell and Brittain in "Art and Belief in Flannery O'Connor," vol. 4, no. 1 (1973), 83–88; on Stephens in vol. 4, no. 3 (1974), 277–78.

19. For fuller treatment of the nature of language and its traditions, see chapter 1.

20. See my "Local Color in *The Awakening*," *The Southern Review*, n.s. 6 (October 1970), 1031–41.

Chapter 1: The New Hermeneutic and the Parables of Jesus

1. For classical presentations of the three generalist approaches to the relationship between religion and literature—heteronomy, autonomy, and theonomy respectively—see T. S. Eliot, "Religion and Literature," in *The New Orpheus: Essays Toward a Christian Poetic,* ed. Nathan A. Scott, Jr. (New York: Sheed & Ward, 1964), pp. 223–35; R. W. B. Lewis, "Hold on Hard to the Huckleberry Bushes," in *Trials of the Word: Essays in American Literature and the Humanistic Tradition* (New Haven: Yale University Press, 1965), pp. 97–111; and Paul Tillich, "Religion and Secular Culture," in *The Protestant Era* (Chicago: University of Chicago Press, 1957), pp. 55–65.

2. Gerhard Ebeling, *Word and Faith* (Philadelphia: Fortress Press, 1963), p. 248.

3. See Bernard J. Cooke, *Christian Sacraments and Christian Personality* (New York: Holt, Rinehart & Winston, 1965); Denis O'Callaghan, *Sacraments, The Gestures of Christ* (New York: Sheed & Ward, 1964); Joseph M. Powers, *Eucharistic Theology* (New York: Herder and Herder, 1967); Karl Rahner, *The Church and the Sacraments* (New York: Herder & Herder, 1963); E. Schillebeeckx, *Christ, the Sacrament of the Encounter with God* (New York: Sheed & Ward, 1963).

4. Ebeling, *Word and Faith*, p. 326.

5. Ibid.

6. Ernst Fuchs, "The New Testament and the Hermeneutical Problem," *The New Hermeneutic*, ed. James M. Robinson and John B. Cobb, Jr. (New York: Harper & Row, 1964), p. 126.

7. Ebeling, *Word and Faith*, p. 318.

8. Robert W. Funk, *Language, Hermeneutic, and Word of God* (New York: Harper & Row, 1966), p. 40.

9. Ibid., p. 39.

10. Boris Eichenbaum, "The Theory of the 'Formal Method,'" *Russian Formalist Criticism: Four Essays,* trans. Lee T. Lemon and Marion J. Reis (Lincoln: University of Nebraska Press, 1965), p. 114, and see Victor Shklovsky, "Art as Technique," ibid., pp. 3–24.

11. O'Connor, *Mystery and Manners: Occasional Prose*, ed. Sally and Robert Fitzgerald (New York: Farrar, Straus & Giroux, 1969), p. 96. Subsequent references in parenthesis refer to the pages of this collection.

12. Ebeling, *Word and Faith*, p. 331.

13. Rene Wellek and Austin Warren, *Theory of Literature*, 3rd ed. (New York: Harcourt, Brace & World, 1962), p. 214.

14. Eliseo Vivas, *Creation and Discovery* (Chicago: Henry Regnery, 1955), p. 87.

15. R. W. B. Lewis, "Hold on Hard to the Huckleberry Bushes," *Sewanee Review* 67 (1959), 477.

16. Sallie McFague TeSelle, *Literature and the Christian Life* (New Haven: Yale University Press, 1966), pp. 70–71.

17. Dan Otto Via, Jr., *The Parables: Their Literary and Existential Dimension* (Philadelphia: Fortress Press, 1967), p. 106.

18. The parables *in the narrow sense* are the Great Wedding Feast (Matt. 22:1–10, Luke 14:16–24), the Prodigal Son (Luke 15:11–32), the Talents (Matt. 25:14–30), the Ten Maidens (Matt. 25:1–13), the Unforgiving Servant (Matt. 18:23–35), the Unjust Steward (Luke 16:1–9), the Wedding Garment (Matt. 22:11–14), the Wicked Tenants (Mark 12:1–11; Matt. 21:33–44; Luke 20:9–18), and the Workers in the Vineyard (Matt. 20:1–16); the *similitudes* are the Barren Fig Tree (Luke 13:6–9), the Budding Fig Tree (Mark 13:28–29; Matt. 24:32–33; Luke 21:29–31), the Children in the Market Place (Matt. 11:16–19; Luke 7:31–35), the Divided House (Mark 3:23–26; Matt. 12:25–26; Luke 11:17–18), the Doorkeeper (Mark 13:33–37; Luke 12:35–38), the Dragnet (Matt. 13:47–50), the Garment Patch and the Old Wineskins (Matt. 9:16–17), the Hidden Treasure (Matt. 13:44), the Leaven (Matt. 13:33; Luke 13:20), the Lost Coin (Luke 15:8–10), the Lost Sheep (Matt. 18:12–14; Luke 15:4–7), the Mustard Seed (Mark 4:30–32), the Pearl Merchant (Matt. 13:45–46), the Seed Growing Secretly (Mark 4:26–29), the Son Asking for Bread (Luke 11:11–13), the Thief at Night (Matt. 24:43–44; Luke 12:39–40), the Tower Builder

and the King Going to War (Luke 14:28–33), the Wheat and the Weeds (Matt. 13:24–30); the *example stories* are the Choice of Place at Table (Luke 14:7–11), the Good Samaritan (Luke 10:30–37), the Importunate Friend (Luke 11:5–10), the Last Judgment (Matt. 25:31–46), the Pharisee and the Publican (Luke 18:9–14), the Rich Fool (Luke 12:16–21), the Rich Man and Lazarus (Luke 16:19–31), the Servant Entrusted with Supervision (Matt. 24:45–51; Luke 12:42–46), the Servant's Reward (Luke 17:7–10), the Two Debtors (Luke 7:41–43), the Two Sons (Matt. 21:28–31), the Unjust Judge (Luke 18:1–8).

19. Via, *The Parables*, p. 11.

20. Ibid., pp. 11–12.

21. Ibid., p. 12.

22. *The New English Bible* (Oxford University Press, Cambridge University Press, 1970).

23. Via, *The Parables*, p. 25.

24. Ibid., pp. 106, 110.

25. O'Connor, *Mystery and Manners*, p. 35.

26. Ibid., p. 113.

27. Funk, *Language, Hermeneutic, and Word of God*, p. 18.

28. Sister Kathleen Feeley, S.S.N.D., *Flannery O'Connor: Voice of the Peacock*, pp. 188–91.

29. Miles Orvell lists the reviews of current works, predominantly theological and scriptural, that O'Connor contributed to her diocesan newspaper between 1956 and 1964 (*Invisible Parade*, pp. 196–99). Among the reviews of other books related to the Bible, he mentions the following: Mircea Eliade, *Patterns in Comparative Religion*; Eric Voegelin, *Israel and Revelation*; J. Guillet, *Themes of the Bible*; F. X. Durrwell, *The Resurrection*; G. E. Wright, ed., *The Bible and the Ancient Near East*; H. H. Rowley, ed., *The Old Testament and Modern Study*; Henri Daniel-Rops, *What is the Bible?*; John J. Heaney, ed., *Faith, Reason, and the Gospels*; Louis J. Putz, ed., *The Kingdom of God: A Short Bible*.

30. Jean Levie, S.J., *The Bible, Word of God in Words of Men* (New York: P. J. Kenedy & Sons, 1961), p. vii; my emphasis.

31. Bruce Vawter, C.M., *The Conscience of Israel: Pre-Exilic Prophets and Prophecy* (New York: Sheed & Ward, 1961), p. 50.

32. Although the question of "objective" evaluation is extraneous to my purpose here, it is nevertheless clear that in addition to its interpretive function, criticism must also eventually perform an evaluative function. It is in this area of evaluation that

the autonomy of literature is most seriously called into question, especially by those who consider literature a mask for doctrine or who have any other disciplinary bias with which they approach literature. In determining what is literature and whether it is great literature, the critic must be extremely cautious and honest concerning the origin of the norms that serve his judgment. If the autonomy of literature is to be preserved, then, the critic will want to avoid both subjecting literature to a set of alien norms and any assumption that would consider literature as fundamentally religious. (Although I obviously prefer an approach to evaluation that respects the autonomy of literature, I recognize the value of heteronomous evaluation, provided the critic is forthright and clear about his presuppositions.)

Critics who evaluate literature on its own terms discuss value in relation to the "aesthetic" nature of literature. Organization and function are crucial for determining what is literature; it is not so much the materials used as the manner in which they are put together and for what purpose. How the critic evaluates literature on purely aesthetic ground has been carefully elucidated by Wellek and Warren. They insist, and rightly so, that the critic need not agree with the *Weltanschauung* of the author; yet they do not say, on the other hand, that the world view of the author is irrelevant to the aesthetic judgment. They modify Eliot's notion that the critic must accept the world view of the work "as coherent, mature, and founded on the facts of experience" (Wellek and Warren, *Theory of Literature*, p. 246). Coherence is already an aesthetic criterion; and maturity, for Wellek and Warren, becomes "inclusiveness" and "awareness of complexity." Moreover, the critic's judgment concerning correspondence with experience is not made on the basis of a simple comparison of the author's world with the critic's experience, as Stephens seems to do. He must compare the work's total world with his own total experience; and the judgment of correspondence "registers itself in aesthetic terms of vividness, intensity, patterned contrast" (ibid.). A work is successful when the materials are completely assimilated into the structure of the work. And the criterion of greatness is "inclusiveness"—the tighter the imaginative integration of diverse materials, the higher the literary value of the work.

There is, however, another evaluative function that the literary critic who is also a theologian may want to perform; and this is to judge whether or not the work is open to a Christian interpretation.

For even if we assert that the ultimate judgment of literature and its greatness must be made according to the aesthetic norm of imaginative integration, it is not contradictory to insist that the *Weltanschauung* of the work can also be judged according to a norm which is extra-aesthetic, if not extraliterary. The aesthetic norm judges the fictional world according to its own inner consistency and coherence; whereas a literary norm implies that, if the theological critic looks for a correspondence between the fictional world and a Christian understanding of reality, he does not expect this correspondence to be expressed in anything other than the language of literature. Thus, he is not looking for theological language, nor will he translate the language of the work into doctrinal statements. He will be searching for a literary analogue of the Christian understanding of man and of the world.

To be considered consonant with Christianity, as O'Connor's fiction obviously is, literature must manifest an openness to the future in the structures of literary affirmation—image and metaphor, plot, character, and setting. It must somehow be an event of promise; it must function integrally as authentic language. For I conceive the radical openness *of* literature to a Christian interpretation to be nothing else than openness *in* literature to the future, an openness based on hope which is central to the Christian proclamation. For there to be hope in literature, the "tone" of the work must steer a middle course between despair and presumption, between Sisyphus and Prometheus. And if literature is to be an event of promise for the reader, it must in its total effect offer him an experience of man as a creature who hopes, who imagines the future, who can sustain present suffering because of the promise that awaits him.

33. O'Connor, *Mystery and Manners*, p. 185.

34. Ibid., pp. 196–97.

35. Ibid., p. 111.

36. Ibid., p. 112.

37. Ibid., p. 102. The original has "the action" for "word." It is clearly no distortion of O'Connor's intentions to make this substitution; *action* for her means word and gesture, as we have seen. In a hermeneutical perspective, *word* is the generic term for all forms of communication, word and gesture included.

38. *The New Testament in Modern English*, trans. J. B. Phillips (New York: Macmillan, 1964), John 15:3.

Chapter 2: The Uncollected Stories

*The qualification "uncollected" is used here to denote those stories not included in the two original collections. All of the stories are, of course, collected in Robert Giroux, ed., *The Complete Stories* (New York, 1971).

1. O'Connor, "The Geranium," an earlier version of the published MS (O'Connor Collection, Milledgeville, Georgia).

2. Generally speaking, O'Connor's natural symbols ("Wildcat," "The Turkey," "The River," the woods in "A View of the Woods," the peacock in "The Displaced Person," the bull in "Greenleaf," and the sky throughout her fiction) somehow seem less appropriate to the hermeneutic structure of her stories and indeed to the parabolic form itself than her man-made symbols (even "The Geranium," but certainly the berth-coffin in "The Train," "The Peeler," the fire in "A Circle in the Fire," "The Artificial Nigger," Hulga's artificial leg in "Good Country People," the tattoo in "Parker's Back," the coffin in "Judgement Day," Haze's car in *Wise Blood*, and bread in *The Violent Bear It Away*).

3. The reference to Haze's sister "Ruby" in "The Peeler" (*The Complete Stories*, p. 78), eliminated from chapter 3 of the novel, is further internal evidence that "A Stroke of Good Fortune" ("A Woman on the Stairs") was originally part of the projected novel that eventually did not fit the overall design.

4. Cf. the contrary interpretation of Hyman, *Flannery O'Connor*, p. 10, and that of Martin, *The True Country*, p. 68.

5. See my *Toward a New Earth: Apocalypse in the American Novel* (Notre Dame, Ind.: University of Notre Dame Press, 1972), pp. 138–39.

6. O'Connor, "The Partridge Pageant," an unpublished earlier version of "The Partridge Festival" (O'Connor Collection, Milledgeville, Georgia).

7. O'Connor, "Why Do the Heathens Rage?" *Esquire* 60 (July, 1963), 60–61. O'Connor dropped the *s* from "Heathens" apparently to avoid association with the fundamentalist advertisement that appears periodically in the Atlanta newspapers.

Chapter 3: The Collections

1. O'Connor, "A Reasonable Use of the Unreasonable," in *Mystery and Manners*, pp. 107–14.

2. Ibid., p. 116.

3. Stephens, *The Question of Flannery O'Connor*, p. 18.

4. Ibid., p. 28.

5. Ibid., p. 24.

6. Orvell, *Invisible Parade*, p. 35.

7. See Albert J. Griffith, "Flannery O'Connor's Salvation Road," *Studies in Short Fiction* 3 (Spring 1966), 329–33.

8. For a balanced appraisal of Mr. Shiftlet's final disposition, eminently supported by evidence from the published version as well as from Mr. Shiftlet's development in revisions of the story, see Charles M. Hegarty, "A Man Though Not Yet a Whole One: Mr. Shiftlet's Genesis," *The Flannery O'Connor Bulletin* 1 (1972), 24–38.

9. Hyman, *Flannery O'Connor*, p. 16.

10. Ibid., p. 19.

11. Stephens, *The Question of Flannery O'Connor*, p. 159.

12. O'Connor, *Mystery and Manners*, p. 27.

13. Martin, *The True Country*, p. 178.

14. See Peter L. Hays, "Dante, Tobit, and 'The Artificial Nigger,'" *Studies in Short Fiction* 5 (Spring 1968), 263–68, and Gilbert H. Muller "The City of Woe: Flannery O'Connor's Dantean Vision," *Georgia Review* 23 (Summer 1969), 206–13.

15. See Turner F. Byrd, "Ironic Dimension in Flannery O'Connor's 'The Artificial Nigger,'" *Mississippi Quarterly* 21 (Fall 1968), 243–51.

16. Orvell, *Invisible Parade*, p. 159.

17. The carbon worksheets of an earlier version of "The Artificial Nigger" show how much more functional the symbol of the statue is in the final version, despite the explicit authorial language of its conclusion, in comparison with the earlier draft's clumsy explanation of the reconciliation it effects. The conclusion of that version follows:

> Mr. Head turned slowly.
>
> Neither Mr. Head nor Nelson ever knew how they were actually reconciled and neither suspected that it was the plaster Negro that did it. Mr. Head thought later that it was the mercy of

God and Nelson didn't like to think about it. They had not gone two blocks toward the station when Mr. Head stopped and stared to the right at something that had caught his eye. He was facing the drive entrance of a yellow brick house set back behind a narrow lawn. There was a low concrete wall around the lawn and at the end of this wall, directly in front of him, sat the painted plaster figure of a Negro man. He was leaning over something as if he were about to take a bite out of it. One of his eyes was entirely white where the paint had peeled off and this gave him an insane look. He was ptiched forward at an unsteady angle because the putty that held him to the wall had cracked. He was about Nelson's size.

Mr. Head stood looking at him silently until Nelson stopped at a little distance. Then as the two of them stood there, Mr. Head breathed, "An artificial nigger!"

It was not possible to tell if he were meant to be young or old; he looked too real to be either. He was meant to look happy because his mouth was stretched up at the corners but the chipped eye and the angle he was cocked at gave him a wild look of misery instead.

"An artificial nigger!" Nelson repeated in Mr. Head's exact tone.

Neither moved.

"They ain't got enough real ones here," Mr. Head said sadly. "They got to have an artificial one."

He put his hand on Nelson's shoulder, with a heavy hesitation, the way he would have felt a stove to see if it were still hot. The boy allowed the hand to stay there and after a minute, they set off again.

Their train glided into the suburb stop just as they reached the station and they boarded it together. Their faces looked almost identical except that Mr. Head's appeared older than it had in the morning and Nelson's looked more wary, as if he had discovered a new enemy even nearer than the one that looked back at him from the train window. They were both afraid the train would not stop and let them off at the junction but it did, just as the moon was beginning to rise, very red and revived, at the bottom of the mountain. (An unpublished version of "The Artificial Nigger," pp. 29–31, O'Connor Collection.)

18. With the proper heuristic principle, one can certainly avoid the poverty of Martha Stephens's recent scruple about the story's

meaning: "Pressed for a statement of its theme, we can do no better than this: Life is dangerous, no one is safe, we all live each day on the verge of misfortune" (*The Question of Flannery O'Connor*, p. 168). Even her later more generous reflection on Sally Virginia's inclusion in the circle of misery lacks precision: "No one can remain a witness to the common plight" (ibid., p. 183).

19. Carter Martin studies the biblical parallel and apparently reaches a different conclusion. "Unlike the biblical king," he writes, "she comes to no revelation as she witnesses the fiery event, for she feels only sorrow, loss, and misery" (*The True Country*, p. 37). The discrepancy in our commentaries doubtlessly lies in how one freights the word "revelation." It seems more accurate theologically, and this has been the pattern of my usage, to distinguish call and response, revelation and conversion.

20. Sister M. Joselyn, O.S.B., "Thematic Centers in 'The Displaced Person,'" *Studies in Short Fiction* 1 (Winter 1964), 85–92.

21. Driskell and Brittain, *The Eternal Crossroads*, pp. 65–66, 75–77.

22. Ibid.,; also Robert Fitzgerald, "The Countryside and the True Country," *Sewanee Review* 70 (Summer 1962), 380–94.

23. See Roy R. Male, "The Two Versions of 'The Displaced Person,'" *Studies in Short Fiction* 7 (Summer 1970), 450–57.

24. Martin, *The True Country*, p. 39.

25. Orvell, *Invisible Parade*, p. 37.

26. Martin, *The True Country*, pp. 231–32.

27. Orvell, *Invisible Parade*, p. 26.

28. Ibid., p. 15.

29. Mr. Fortune does not drown, as Driskell and Brittain conclude (*The Eternal Crossroads*, p. 29); it is the convulsive expansion of his heart that makes him feel "*as if* he were being pulled after it through the woods" and "*as if* he were running as fast as he could with the ugly pines toward the lake" (my emphases).

30. Cf. Sister M. Bernetta Quinn, O.S.F., "Flannery O'Connor, a Realist of Distances," in *The Added Dimension,* ed. Melvin J. Friedman and Lewis A. Lawson (New York: Fordham University Press, 1966), p. 161. There is no apparent literary or theological justification for the type of conclusion that Sister M. Bernetta draws. "Whatever the sheriff or others may think, Thomas's mother has not died in vain," she writes. "Thomas has put his hand into the Lord's wounded side."

31. Orvell, *Invisible Parade*, p. 166. Orvell's emphasis in analysis

rests heavily on Farebrother's satisfied expectations and on the mother's indignation at the thought of Thomas's having put a gun in Sarah's purse, but even here it seems that promiscuity rather than sexuality is the object of the satire—and there is, for me at least, an obvious difference between the two.

32. Ibid.

33. Charles M. Hegarty, S.J., review of Driskell and Brittain, *The Eternal Crossroads*, in *Studies in Short Fiction* 10 (1973), 120. Hegarty takes strong exception to Driskell's and Brittain's reading of the next to last paragraph of "The Lame Shall Enter First" as conclusive proof of Sheppard's lingering "immorality." Although there is evidence elsewhere in *The Eternal Crossroads*, as Hegarty carefully documents, that Driskell and Brittain had not resolved completely their own uncertainties about the text (*The Eternal Crossroads*, pp. 94, 132), they conclude that "if any doubt of Sheppard's immorality remains, he stands convicted in these few lines; his love for the child is totally selfish: he would use the boy to 'transfuse' life into himself" (ibid., p. 98). Hegarty rejects their judgment on the grounds that "it ignores the context of the final scene, calls upon other fictional scenes of Flannery O'Connor to illuminate it, and is ultimately an intense misreading of the text." When he turns to his own brief justification of his assertion that "the scene is one of classical tragic recognition," he says simply that in the description of the crucial paragraph "Sheppard is deliberately shown in this light (i.e., as one who 'realizes he has stuffed his own emptiness with good works') as a fitting prelude to his vision of his dead son, his vision of the light that purges as it illuminates." There is, moreover, evidence enough to show that Hegarty is hoist by his own petard when he accuses them of ignoring the scene's context.

34. Two earlier versions of the story found in the O'Connor Collection demonstrate clearly how O'Connor was gradually amplifying the description of Sheppard's final messianic illusion. The progressive exaggeration of the controverted reaction is evident as follows:

(1) A rush of love for the child swept over him. He jumped up and ran to his room to kiss him, to tell him that he loved him, that he would *not* fail him again. [The "not" becomes "never."]

(2) A rush of agonizing love for the child swept over him. He would make *it* up to him! He would never let him suffer again! He would be mother and father. He jumped up and ran to his

room, to kiss him, to tell him that he loved him, that he would never fail him again. [Note here the "it" for the more emphatic and universal "everything" of the published MS.]

Moreover, in these two earlier versions, Sheppard's pain preceding the appearances of metanoia is described as "guilt"; the published MS changes "guilt" to "repulsion," reducing significantly the religious implications of the experience. The unpublished variations precede the final version here: (1) "He fell back stunned. He felt the pain of a guilt so clear and intense that he gasped for breath." (2) "His heart constricted with the pain of a guilt so clear and intense that he gasped for breath." (3) "His heart constricted with a repulsion for himself so clear and intense that he gasped for breath."

35. Forrest L. Ingram, "O'Connor's Seven-Story Cycle," *The Flannery O'Connor Bulletin* 2 (1973), 19–28.

36. As explicit as the story is about the source of its "revelation," not every critic has been willing to take its allusions at face value. In view of the quality of Ruby's final vision, her emphasis on gratitude to God, the simile that has her "defending her innocence to invisible guests who were like the comforters of Job," and the repeated though noncapitalized references to "you" in Ruby's monologue, Josephine Hendin seems unnecessarily reserved in saying that Ruby "shouts . . . to her fields," rather than at God as she actually does (Hendin, *The World of Flannery O'Connor*, p. 119).

37. A few deft changes to the conclusion of the story once again demonstrate how O'Connor's revisions repeatedly strengthened the interpretive structure of her stories and clarified the nature of the protagonist's response. In an earlier version of "Revelation," Ruby returns to the house *before* her vision; the last paragraph of that version follows:

Until the sun slipped finally behind the tree line she remained there with her gaze bent to them. Then she got down and turned off the faucet and made her way on the darkening path to the house. By the time she reached her back door and looked behind her, there was only a purple streak in the sky, like an extension of the highway leading into the night, but a visionary light had settled in her eyes. She saw the streak as a vast swinging bridge extending upward from the earth. Upon it a hoard of souls rumbled toward heaven. There were whole companies of white-trash, clean for the first time in their lives, and bands of black niggers in white robes, and battalions of freaks and lunatics shouting and clapping and leaping like frogs. And coming behind all of them was a tribe of people whom she recognized at once as those who, like herself and Claud, had always had a little of everything and the God-given wit to use it right. They were marching behind the others with great dignity, *driving them, in fact, ahead of themselves*, still responsible as they had always been for good order and common sense and respectable behavior. *They walked upright as they had done in life, their eyes small but fixed unblinkingly on what lay ahead.* And the whole hoard was shouting halleluja. (An earlier version of the published MS, pp. 27–28, O'Connor Collection, my emphases.)

Although Ruby's "tribe" is bringing up the rear of the procession, their appearance is far less subdued than in the final version (note italicized portions), and their eyes rather than Ruby's are "fixed unblinkingly on what lay ahead." The published version emphasizes the relationship between the vision and Ruby's status as "wart hog" by having her remain at the pig parlor during the revelation and return "to the house" only after the "abysmal life-giving knowledge" has been "absorbed."

38. Martin, *The True Country*, p. 130.

39. Melvin J. Friedman, "Introduction," in *The Added Dimension*, ed. Friedman and Lawson, p. 22.

40. The MS variations in order of appearance are as follows: (1) "The sun began to emerge, a tree of fire, facing the dark where Parker was." (2) "A tree of fire, slowly, majestically, began to ascend, facing the dark where Parker was." (3) "A tree of fire, slowly majestically, began to ascend, facing the dark where Parker was." (4) "Slowly majestically, as he stared, a tree of fire ascended." (5) ". . . and the sun, a tree of fire, majestically ascended."

41. The imagery of Parker's experience of transformation went through the following instructive stages of revision: (1) "He felt like some fragile thing of nature, a peacock or a butterfly, but more wondrous an arabesque of color that only himself and the Lord could see." (2) "He felt like some fragile thing of nature, turned into an arabesque of colors that only himself and the Lord could see." (3) "He felt like some fragile thing of nature, turned into an arabesque of colors." (4) "He felt like some fragile thing of nature, turned by the light into a perfect arabesque of colors that only himself and the Lord could see." (5) "He felt like some fragile thing of nature, turned by the light into a perfect arabesque of colors. He knew, with a knowledge born of nothing, that only himself and the

Lord could see them." (6) "Parker felt the light pouring through his spider-web soul turning it into a perfect arabesque of colors, a garden of paradise where the panther and the lion and the serpent and the hawk . . ." (7) " 'Obadiah,' he whispered and all at once he felt the light pouring through his spider-web soul turning it into a perfect arabesque of colors, a garden of trees and birds and beasts."

42. MS variations of the final sentence appear in the following order: (1) "Outside he leaned against the trunk of the pecan tree and cried like a baby." (2) "Outside Parker leaned against the trunk of the pecan tree and wept." (3) "There he was leaning against the trunk of the pine tree, crying like a baby." *Deleted additional sentence*: "She turned and went into the house and began to make her preparations to leave." (4) "She looked toward the pecan tree and there he was, leaning against it, crying like a baby." *Handcorrected to read*: "She looked toward the pecan tree and her gimlet eyes hardened: there he was, leaning against it, crying like a baby." (5) "There he was—who called himself Obadiah Elihue—leaning against the tree, crying like a baby."

43. Robert Giroux, "Introduction," in Flannery O'Connor, *The Complete Stories* (New York: Farrar, Straus & Giroux, 1971), p. xvi.

44. Two transitional versions of the story entitled "Getting Home" reveal final paragraphs that simply project old Fairlee's return home in death into his daughter's victory in argument (the name Tanner has not yet appeared). They follow in order of revision:

> (1) She and her husband had an extended argument over where he should be buried. He said here. She said at home. And she won. She wanted to rest at night and he was just the kind, she said, who if she didn't follow his instructions to the letter, would haunt her the rest of her days.

> (2) She and her husband had an extended argument over the telephone about where he should be buried. He said here. She said at home. And she won. She wanted to rest at night, and if she didn't follow his instructions to the letter, he was just the kind, she said, who would haunt her the rest of her life.

The changes in the second ending are minor and show no advancement whatever in O'Connor's conception of the old man's victory. The next three drafts leading to the published version (the first of which has "Judgement Day" handwritten in place of the deleted "Getting Home") all have variations of the final ending in which Tanner actually returns home; it is his influence over his daughter *after* death—similar to Addie Bundren's domination of her family in death in *As I Lay Dying*—rather than the daughter's anticipation of his continued influence that affects her change in plans.

(3) She buried him in New York City but after she had done it, she could not sleep at night, so she had him dug up and shipped the body to Corinth. And now she rests well at night, which at her time of life is essential.

(4) She buried him in New York City, but after she had done it she could not sleep at night. Night after night she turned and tossed and very definite lines began to appear in her face, so she had him dug up and shipped the body to Corinth and now she rests well at night. [*Corrected by hand to read*: . . . Corinth. Now she rests well at night and her good looks have mostly returned.]

(5) [*The same as 4 with this grammatical change in the second to last sentence*;] . . . so she had him dug up and the body shipped to Corinth. . . .

The published story, of course, conforms exactly to variation 4 as corrected by hand. Although the grammatical change from 4 to 5 seems minor, the latter actually has the effect of separating old Tanner from his body, a theological implication that O'Connor wanted to avoid perhaps in returning to the former wording. What these three revisions and final version emphasize significantly that the earlier two did not is how the daughter's decision is blatantly self-serving, how Tanner's influence is felt even in death, but most importantly how his symbolic victory yields *actual* homecoming.

45. Martin, *The True Country*, p. 27.
46. Ibid.

Chapter 4: The Novels

1. Feeley, *Flannery O'Connor: The Voice of the Peacock*, p. 57.
2. Ibid., p. 58.
3. Ibid.
4. George Ferguson, *Signs and Symbols in Christian Art* (New York: Oxford University Press, 1961), p. 154.

5. We have already discussed implications of Enoch's threefold
initiation into the mystery of the museum in analyzing "The Heart
of the Park," which was revised only slightly to become chapter 5 of
the novel. Other instances in the story and chapter include the
"three women . . . with their suits split," "the woman with the two
little boys"; Haze drives around the pool "a third time" before
stopping; Enoch thinks that Hawks's address "begins with a three"
(in the story it begins with a "two"); the "undersmell" in the
museum hall is a "third" odor; there are "three coffin-like" glass
cases in the middle of the third room, the mummy is in the "third"
case with "three bowls" in front of it; he is "three feet long";
finally, city, park, and museum represent three concentric circles of
deepening significance. Chapter 8 continues the magical pattern of
three's: there are three pieces of furniture in Enoch's room and three
pictures on the wall; the washstand is "built in three parts"; Enoch
performs another ritual in three stages—buys popcorn from a
machine, gets a Lime-Cherry Surprise in a drug store, and goes to the
movies for a triple feature; and "two or three" people leave the car
where Haze is preaching the equality of the "three crosses" on
Calvary.

6. Hyman, *Flannery O'Connor*, p. 37.

7. See Martin, *The True Country*, pp. 124–25, and Orvell,
Invisible Parade, p. 84.

8. See Robert Detweiler, "The Curse of Christ in Flannery
O'Connor's Fiction," *Comparative Literature Studies* 3 (1966), 241,
245 n. 7, for a discussion of negative evidence related to the
question of Haze's redemption. Detweiler understandably rejects the
excess of Jonathan Baumbach's interpretation of Haze's redemption
as exemplary ("The Acid of God's Grace: The Fiction of Flannery
O'Connor," *Georgia Review* 17 [Fall 1963], 334).

9. Regarding the meaning of the title there has been a fairly
unanimous consensus, even though the language of the critics often
seems contradictory. Hyman says that "Haze, in the author's view,
really *has* wise blood; the blood of his grandfather, the inherited
vocation, that preaches *through him* Christ's Blood, shed to redeem"
(*Flannery O'Connor*, p. 11), but apparently intends little more than
Martha Stephens, who observes more cautiously, "The title concept
of the book is clearly an ironical one—one's blood is not 'wise'; to
believe that it is (that one can rely simply on self) is the classic
fundamental error of prideful mankind" (*The Question of Flannery
O'Connor*, p. 55).

10. See my *Toward a New Earth*, pp. 134–38.

11. This distinction alone would seem adequate for questioning the severity of Louis D. Rubin's interpretation of the price that Tarwater must pay to believe: "the denial and utter extinction of the possibility of love" ("Flannery O'Connor and the Bible Belt," in *The Curious Death of the Novel: Essays in American Literature* [Baton Rouge: Louisiana State University Press, 1967], p. 256).

12. O'Connor, *Mystery and Manners*, p. 102; also see above, chapter 1, n. 37.

A Selected
Bibliography of Textual
Analyses

I. THE COMPLETE STORIES

Burns, Stuart L. "Flannery O'Connor's Literary Apprenticeship." *Renascence* 22 (Autumn 1969), 3–16.

Martin, Carter W. "Flannery O'Connor's Early Fiction." *Southern Humanities Review* 7 (Spring 1973), 210–14.

A. *A Good Man Is Hard to Find*

"A Good Man Is Hard to Find"

Doxey, William S. "A Dissenting Opinion of Flannery O'Connor's 'A Good Man is Hard to Find.' " *Studies in Short Fiction* 10 (Spring 1973), 199–204.

Kropf, C.F. "Theme and Setting in 'A Good Man is Hard to Find.' " *Renascence* 24 (Summer 1972), 177–80, 206.

Marks, W.S., III. "Advertisements for Grace: Flannery O'Connor's 'A Good Man is Hard to Find.' " *Studies in Short Fiction* 4 (Fall 1966), 19–27.

Montgomery, Marion. "Miss Flannery's 'Good Man.' " *Denver Quarterly* 3 (Autumn 1968), 1–19.

"The Life You Save May Be Your Own"

Griffith, Albert J. "Flannery O'Connor's Salvation Road." *Studies in Short Fiction* 3 (Spring 1966), 329–33.

Hegarty, Charles M., S.J. "A Man Though Not Yet a Whole One: Mr. Shiftlet's Genesis." *The Flannery O'Connor Bulletin* 1 (Autumn 1972), 24–38.

"A Stroke of Good Fortune" ("A Woman On The Stairs")

Montgomery, Marion. "Flannery O'Connor's 'Leaden Tract Against Complacency and Contraception.'" *Arizona Quarterly* 24 (Summer 1968), 133–146.

"A Temple of the Holy Ghost"

Bassan, Maurice. "Flannery O'Connor's Way: Shock, with Moral Intent." *Renascence* 15 (Summer 1963), 195–99, 211.

Mayer, David R. "Apologia for the Imagination: Flannery O'Connor's 'A Temple of the Holy Ghost.'" *Studies in Short Fiction* 11 (Spring 1974), 147–52.

"The Artificial Nigger"

Byrd, Turner F. "Ironic Dimension in Flannery O'Connor's 'The Artificial Nigger.'" *Mississippi Quarterly* 21 (Fall 1968), 243–51.

Hays, Peter L. "Dante, Tobit, and 'The Artificial Nigger.'" *Studies in Short Fiction* 5 (Spring 1968), 263–68.

Muller, Gilbert H. "The City of Woe: Flannery O'Connor's Dantean Vision." *Georgia Review* 23 (Summer 1969), 206–13.

"Good Country People"

Jones, Bartlett C. "Depth Psychology and Literary Study." *Mid-Continent American Studies Journal* 5 (Fall 1964), 50–56.

"The Displaced Person"

Fitzgerald, Robert. "The Countryside and the True Country." *Sewanee Review* 70 (Summer 1962), 380–94.

Joselyn, Sister M., O.S.B. "Thematic Centers in 'The Displaced Person.'" *Studies in Short Fiction* 1 (Winter 1964), 85–92.

Male, Roy R. "The Two Versions of 'The Displaced Person.'" *Studies in Short Fiction* 7 (Summer 1970), 450–57.

B. *Everything That Rises Must Converge*

Driskell, Leon. " 'Parker's Back' vs 'The Partridge Festival': Flannery O'Connor's Critical Choice." *Georgia Review* 21 (Winter 1967), 476–90.

Ingram, Forrest L. "O'Connor's Seven-Story Cycle." *The Flannery O'Connor Bulletin* 2 (Autumn 1973), 19–28.

"Everything That Rises Must Converge"

Desmond, John F. "The Lessons of History: Flannery O'Connor's 'Everything That Rises Must Converge.' " *The Flannery O'Connor Bulletin* 1 (Autumn 1972), 39–45.

Maida, Patricia Dinneen. " 'Convergence' in Flannery O'Connor's 'Everything That Rises Must Converge.' " *Studies in Short Fiction* 7 (Fall 1970), 549–55.

Montgomery, Marion. "On Flannery O'Connor's 'Everything That Rises Must Converge.' " *Critique* 13:2 (1971), 15–29.

"Greenleaf"

Asals, Frederick. "The Mythic Dimensions of Flannery O'Connor's 'Greenleaf.' " *Studies in Short Fiction* 5 (Summer 1968), 317–30.

"A View of the Woods"

Riso, Don, S.J. "Blood and Land in 'A View of the Woods.' " *New Orleans Review* 1 (Spring 1969), 255–57.

"The Comforts of Home"

Millichap, Joseph R. "The Pauline 'Old Man' in Flannery O'Connor's 'The Comforts of Home.' " *Studies in Short Fiction* 11 (Winter 1974), 96–99.

"The Lame Shall Enter First"

Asals, Frederick. "Flannery O'Connor's 'The Lame Shall Enter First.' " *Mississippi Quarterly* 23 (Spring 1970), 103–20.

Spivey, Ted Ray. "Flannery O'Connor's Views of God and Man." *Studies in Short Fiction* 1 (Spring 1964), 200–206.

"Parker's Back"

Browing, Preston M., Jr. " 'Parker's Back': Flannery O'Connor's Iconography of Salvation by Profanity." *Studies in Short Fiction* 6 (Fall 1969), 525–35.

Fahey, William A. "Flannery O'Connor's 'Parker's Back.' " *Renascence* 20 (Spring 1968), 162–64, 166.

Gordon, Caroline. "Heresy in Dixie." *Sewanee Review* 76 (Spring 1968), 261–97.

"Judgement Day"

Howell, Elmo. "Flannery O'Connor and the Home Country." *Renascence* 24 (Summer 1972), 171–76.

II. THE NOVELS

A. *Wise Blood*

Asals, Frederick. "The Road to *Wise Blood*." *Renascence* 21 (Summer 1969), 181–94.

Baumbach, Jonathan. "The Acid of God's Grace: The Fiction of Flannery O'Connor." *Georgia Review* 17 (Fall 1963), 334–46.

Burns, Stuart L. "The Evolution of *Wise Blood*." *Modern Fiction Studies* 16 (Summer 1970), 147–62.

Burns, Stuart L. "Structural Patterns in *Wise Blood*." *Xavier University Studies* 8 (Summer 1969), 32–43.

Harrison, Margaret. "Hazel Motes in Transit: A Comparison of Two Versions of Flannery O'Connor's 'The Train' with Chapter I of *Wise Blood*." *Studies in Short Fiction* 8 (Spring 1971), 287–93.

Littlefield, Daniel F., Jr. "Flannery O'Connor's *Wise Blood*: 'Unparalleled Prosperity' and Spiritual Chaos." *Mississippi Quarterly* 23 (Spring 1970), 121–33.

McCullagh, James C. "Symbolism and the Religious Aesthetic: Flannery O'Connor's *Wise Blood*." *The Flannery O'Connor Bulletin* 2 (Autumn 1973), 43–58.

Rechnitz, Robert M. "Passionate Pilgrim: Flannery O'Connor's *Wise Blood*." *Georgia Review* 19 (Fall 1965), 310–16.

B. *The Violent Bear It Away*

Burns, Stuart L. "Flannery O'Connor's *The Violent Bear It Away*: Apotheosis in Failure." *Sewanee Review* 76 (Spring 1968), 319–36.

Eggenschwiler, David. "Flannery O'Connor's True and False Prophets." *Renascence* 21 (Spring 1969), 151–61, 167.

Fahey, William A. "Out of the Eater: Flannery O'Connor's Appetite for Truth." *Renascence* 20 (Autumn 1967), 22–29.

McCown, Robert M., S.J. "The Education of a Prophet: A Study of Flannery O'Connor's *The Violent Bear It Away*." *Kansas Magazine* (1962), 73–78.

Mayer, David R. "*The Violent Bear It Away*: Flannery O'Connor's Shaman." *The Southern Literary Journal* 4 (Spring 1972), 41–54.

Nolde, Sister M. Simon, O.S.B. "*The Violent Bear It Away*: A Study in Imagery." *Xavier University Studies* 1 (Spring 1962), 180–94.

Trowbridge, Clinton W. "The Symbolic Vision of Flannery O'Connor: Patterns of Imagery in *The Violent Bear It Away*." *Sewanee Review* 76 (Spring 1968), 298–318.

Index